SECRET OKLAHOMA

A Guide to the Weird, Wonderful, and Obscure

Matt Kirouac

REEDY PRESS

Reedy Press
PO Box 5131
St. Louis, MO 63139
reedypress.com

Library of Congress Control Number: 2025936318
ISBN: 9781681066158

Design by Jill Halpin

Unless otherwise indicated, all photos are courtesy of the author
or in the public domain.

Printed in the United States of America
25 26 27 28 29   5 4 3 2 1

DEDICATION

To my husband, Nathan, my favorite Oklahoman.
Thank you for making Oklahoma a home.

Ed Galloway's Totem Pole Park contains the tallest concrete totem pole in the world and has become a Route 66 staple. Courtesy of Lori Duckworth/Oklahoma Tourism

CONTENTS

ACKNOWLEDGMENTS

I never would have come to Oklahoma if it weren't for my sister-in-law, Whitney. I remember when my brother told me about his new (at the time) girlfriend, and that she was from Oklahoma. I was weirdly delighted and intrigued, considering it was one of the few states I hadn't yet visited, and frankly I knew basically nothing about it. I was so intrigued, in fact, that I essentially invited myself on their next trip to Oklahoma to visit Whitney's family. What I expected when I first visited in 2017, and what I discovered, were wildly different. That trip was so formative that it paved the way to me settling here, after traveling the country for two years in an RV, eager to plant roots in a new city I loved. A lot of that is a testament to Oklahomans themselves, some of the most welcoming people I've ever met, as well as those who made me feel like family. I wouldn't be here if it weren't for Whitney and her family, especially Chris, Kelly, and Lindsey. They made this place a home. I'm also grateful for meeting some of the best friends of my life: Selisha, Nick, Josh, Justine, Julie, Clayton, and Jessica. For all the laughs, hugs, and support, you make this place a home. Most importantly, I want to thank my husband, Nathan. When I was going through a divorce and planning on leaving, I met you when I was meant to, and my life here has been better for it. I love you.

INTRODUCTION

Growing up in New Hampshire and Chicago, I never knew much about Oklahoma, aside from stereotypical presumptions about tornadoes, chicken-fried steak, and wind sweeping down the plains. But upon visiting for the first time in 2017, to meet my sister-in-law's family who lives just outside of Oklahoma City, I was blown away not by wind—but by how staggeringly unexpected, exciting, and original this "flyover" state is. An epicenter of discovery and distinction, the Sooner State is one of unabashed weirdness that defies stereotypes at every turn, from its surprisingly rugged topography in the Wichita Mountains and the *Dune*-like atmosphere of Little Sahara State Park to its endless Route 66 kitsch, its Pride festivals, its arts scene, and its tasting-menu restaurants in Oklahoma City, Tulsa, and on farmland in between. Not quite the Midwest, not quite the South, and not quite the Southwest, Oklahoma is hard to pinpoint not just on a map, but in every aspect. From its cuisine and its Mother Road to its Indigenous heritage and museums dedicated to rattlesnakes, pigeons, and the *Twister* movie, there are so many secrets to share from this great state in the Great Plains.

OKLAHOMA'S OWN JOHN WILKES BOOTH

Did Abraham Lincoln's killer actually die in Enid?

On the morning of January 13, 1903, a house painter named David E. George died by his own hand by way of arsenic poisoning in room four of the Grand Avenue Hotel in Enid. Tragic, yes, but otherwise an unremarkable blip in Oklahoma lore . . . aside from the theory that the man was actually President Lincoln's assassin, John Wilkes Booth, using a pseudonym and disguise.

Accepted history has it that, after shooting the president at Ford's Theatre in DC, Booth himself was shot in the head by Sgt. Boston Corbett at the Garrett farm in Virginia. Corbett defied orders to capture the criminal alive. He identified the body as Booth's, and this was later confirmed in an autopsy, but considering the antiquated science of autopsies in 1865, and Booth's skills as an escape artist and actor, rumors began circulating that he had actually evaded detection and made his way to pre-statehood Oklahoma Territory for anonymity.

GRAND AVENUE HOTEL

WHAT: John Wilkes Booth may or may not haunt this former hotel.

WHERE: 205 S Grand Ave., Enid

COST: Free

PRO TIP: For more Booth conspiracy theorizing, read *The Escape and Suicide of John Wilkes Booth*, by Finis L. Bates.

In a shocking coincidence, Booth's killer, Sgt. Boston Corbett, just so happens to be buried in Enid.

After George's death, though, pieces started puzzling together. No one in Enid knew the man, and a coroner's jury heard reports of his lackluster painting skills and his frequent drinking, which might explain him being quoted as saying, "I killed the best man that ever lived." His embalmed body was placed in the front window of a funeral home, and rumors began to swirl of his resemblance to Booth—a rumor stoked by Memphis lawyer Finis L. Bates, who identified the body as his friend John St. Helen. During said friendship, St. Helen had allegedly confessed to Bates that he was actually Booth, providing details about the assassination and his evasion.

Whatever his moniker, be it Booth or George or St. Helen, his mummified body was passed around fairs and carnivals before disappearing to time. The present-day Garfield Furniture store that stands where Grand Avenue Hotel once was is said to be haunted by Booth's ghost.

Courtesy of Oklahoma Historical Society

THE NATION'S CAPITAL OF ALL-BLACK TOWNS

BOLEY HISTORIC DISTRICT

WHAT: Booker T. Washington called Boley "the most enterprising and . . . interesting" all-black town.

WHERE: Main St., Boley

COST: Guided tours are available for a fee.

PRO TIP: Boley Tours also operates a coffee and souvenir shop, and guided hayride tours encompass 14 landmarks.

Courtesy of Nicol Ragland

What made Oklahoma the "Promised Land"?

When most folks envision Oklahomans, they think of cowboys, Native tribes, and Wild West bacchanalia. But a sizable portion of the state is rooted in black culture—namely, between 1865 and 1920, Oklahoma was home to more all-black towns than anywhere else in the US.

Around the turn of the 20th century, there were more than 50 all-black settlements throughout the pre-statehood territory, many founded by formerly enslaved black people who migrated westward with Indigenous tribes during the Trail of Tears. Numbering more than any other US state, these towns proliferated after the Civil War, when former slaves (aka "Freemen") living with tribes like the Choctaw, Chickasaw, Cherokee, and Seminole banded together for camaraderie and protection. Newly free of enslavement and racial prejudice, these communities enabled residents to exist in peace and solidarity, opening their own businesses,

Photos courtesy of Nicol Ragland

schools, and farmland. These settlements expanded with the Land Run of 1889, when black settlers claimed their own homesteads during the mad dash into Oklahoma Territory.

Towns like Lincoln, Cimarron City, Bailey, Zion, Emanuel, Udora, and Douglas all thrived for periods of time as havens of black culture and heritage. Following statehood in 1907, however, Jim Crow laws saw the demise of many of these towns via enforced segregation, with many black residents opting to leave the state for greener pastures westward. The Great Depression, coupled with the closure of numerous railroads throughout the 1930s, effectively cut off rural towns and stifled their economies.

Most all-black towns are a thing of the past in Oklahoma, but 13 remain—like Langston, Boley, Brooksville, Clearview, Lima, and Vernon—as a glimpse of living history and a facet of state history that is often overlooked.

Located 70 miles east of Oklahoma City, Boley is the largest remaining all-black town. Founded in 1903, with about 1,100 residents in a 1.6-square-mile area, its historic district is available for guided or self-guided tours.

Courtesy Oklahoma Historical Society

WEALTH, INFAMY, AND THE FBI

What led the "richest people on Earth" into a "Reign of Terror"?

Wealth has long been a guiding—or misguiding—light in the story of American prosperity. It's what led to numerous gold rushes and boomtowns, to colonization and expansion. It also led to an infamous era in American history known as the "Reign of Terror."

Not nearly as widely known as it should be, despite the fact that one of the most famed directors in the world made a blockbuster about it in 2023, the reign was a greed-driven blight that befell the Osage Nation in the 1920s. Oil was discovered on their land in northeastern Oklahoma after the tribes were forced to move south from Kansas—their third displacement in less than 50 years. The prosperous find, however, quickly devolved from good fortune to a curse, as money-hungry settlers manipulated and murdered members of the Osage to capitalize on the newfound "black gold."

Osage headright holders, those who earned royalties from any oil drilled in their nation, became the richest people, per

---

The oil nickname "Black Gold" entered the national lexicon when an Osage-bred horse by that name won the Kentucky Derby in 1924.

Photos courtesy of Lori Duckworth/Oklahoma Tourism

capita, in the world. Such an unprecedented turn of events led to the "Reign of Terror" in the 1920s, when white settlers married into Osage families and took out life insurance policies to gain a share of headrights. It also led to the creation of the Federal Bureau of Investigation (FBI). Dozens of mysterious deaths occurred during this time, linked to the likes of William King Hale and Ernest Burkhart, prompting the first homicide case for the newly formed FBI.

Killers of the Flower Moon, a book by David Grann and an adapted movie by Martin Scorsese, brought newfound attention to the Reign of Terror, spotlighting a nation of prosperous, proud people. Today, there are about 21,000 members of the Osage Nation, with about half the population still in Oklahoma, and many still receive royalty payments for oil. Headquartered in the town of Pawhuska, attractions include the Osage Nation Museum, which dates to 1938.

OSAGE NATION MUSEUM

WHAT: The oldest tribally governed museum in the country tells the story of the Osage Nation.

WHERE: 819 Grandview Ave., Pawhuska

COST: Free

PRO TIP: Venture into the town of Hominy to marvel at Osage art by the likes of Cha' Tullis, an Indigenous artist whose work features on murals and his namesake Cha' Tullis Gallery.

THE REAL MAN BEHIND *OKLAHOMA!*

Who inspired Rodgers and Hammerstein's most famed musical?

Legends were born in the town of Claremore. Located on Route 66, it's home to the largest privately owned gun collection at the J. M. Davis Arms & Historical Museum, as well as the Will Rogers Memorial Museum—commemorating Oklahoma's "favorite son." The town was also the birthplace of a lesser-known Oklahoma son: Rollie Lynn Riggs. While most people associate *Oklahoma!* as a play from Rodgers and Hammerstein, the iconic musical owes a debt to a native Oklahoman. Rollie Lynn Riggs was born in the town of Claremore in 1899. The part-Cherokee, closeted gay man would grow up to become a prosperous—albeit underrated—playwright, and Claremore's native son, responsible for cultural contributions like *Knives from Syria*, *The Cherokee Night*, and *Green Grow the Lilacs*. The latter was adapted into *Oklahoma!*, a theatrical sensation that not only served as Rodgers and Hammerstein's magnum opus but also forever shifted the paradigm of modern musicals.

Growing up in rural Oklahoma as a closeted gay man meant Riggs spent most of his life roving the world, seeking places that felt inspiring and safe. He lived in Santa Fe, Paris, and Chicago, but he frequently used his home state as source material. Thus were planted the seeds for *Green Grow the Lilacs*, a 1931 play about farmers living in Indian Territory, and a love triangle

---

Despite his nickname, "Broadway's Forgotten Man," Riggs was properly honored in death, marking the first time in state history a governor sent a state flag to be draped over a coffin.

between Curly, Laurey, and Jeeter. Some characters, like Aunt Eller, were inspired by Riggs's own family members.

The play opened to lukewarm success at New York City's Guild Theatre in 1931, running a mere 64 shows. However, it received a fresh windfall of success when Riggs was drafted into the army in 1942 and gave Rodgers and Hammerstein the script, which they were interested in adapting. Slight tweaks were made, but most of Riggs's writing remained. After premiering in 1943, *Oklahoma!* was an instant, sold-out success, going on to become one of the most famed and successful musicals of all time. The first musical for Rodgers and Hammerstein, *Oklahoma!* changed the way musicals were performed by focusing on a narrative story. Riggs disappeared into comparative anonymity. He was well paid for his source material, but outside of the hometown he so often referenced, he remains the mystery man behind one of the world's most significant musicals.

CLAREMORE MUSEUM OF HISTORY

WHAT: The birthplace of the modern musical

WHERE: 121 N Weenonah Ave., Claremore

COST: Free

PRO TIP: Be sure to pose with the Lynn Riggs statue outside the museum, then tune in to the bi-monthly Claremore Museum of History podcast, *The MoH You Know*, to learn more.

Courtesy of Claremore Museum of History

THE ACTION FIGURE MUSEUM THAT SAVED A TOWN

What brought Barbie, Superman, and the Simpsons to Pauls Valley?

Forget Malibu and Metropolis; the real epicenter of Barbie dolls and superheroes is Pauls Valley, Oklahoma. The otherwise nondescript town looks like every other Mayberry stand-in at a glance, but one striking storefront holds a world of pop culture nostalgia that spans decades, genres, and mediums.

The Toy & Action Figure Museum, upon opening in 2005, became the first in the world dedicated to the art of action figures. It's a passion project for Kevin Stark, a local artist and toy designer who serves as the museum's curator, and whose work includes the Teenage Mutant Ninja Turtles and Zorro. And in true superhero form, the museum was a boon to the local economy, conceptualized during citywide discussion in 2000 to turn Pauls Valley into a destination. In seeking out attractions not found elsewhere, the community rallied behind a toy and action figure museum—the likes of which don't exist on this scale anywhere else in the world.

The nonprofit museum leaned on Stark's connections and collections to flesh out a space brimming with more nostalgia than Disneyland. Altogether, the museum contains more than

THE TOY & ACTION FIGURE MUSEUM

WHAT: Pop culture nostalgia on full display

WHERE: 111 S Chickasaw St., Pauls Valley

COST: Small fee for entry, free for children 2 and under

PRO TIP: Museum founder and collector Kevin Stark has his own art gallery down the street, the Stark Art Studio & Gallery.

Photos courtesy of Lori Duckworth/Oklahoma Tourism

13,000 action figures and toys, from comic book iconography and rare Barbies to esoteric characters, *Simpsons* displays, and entire rooms dedicated to Star Wars, Batman, and G. I. Joe. One feature is the Collector's Bedroom, where nearly every square inch is filled with toys and action figures, from Spider-Man and *Toy Story* to Superman, the Hulk, and *Jurassic Park* dinosaurs. Along the way, the museum weaves history and stories through its exhibits, along with videos, props, vintage cereal boxes, and PEZ dispensers.

The town's goal of establishing a destination paid off. The Toy & Action Figure Museum has been named one of *Time* magazine's "50 Most Authentic American Experiences" and has seen visitors from every state in the country, plus more than 40 other countries, for a total of more than 50,000 travelers and counting.

The museum also contains the Oklahoma Cartoonists Collection, a comic-centric wing with thousands of items from Oklahomans like Pulitzer-winning Bill Mauldin, and Chester Gould of *Dick Tracy* fame.

AMERICA'S MOST UNDERRATED BURGER

How did the Great Depression lead to one of America's most unique burgers?

Every May, as equestrians don their best hats for the Kentucky Derby, another kind of festival in Oklahoma celebrates the largest onion burger in the world. The Fried Onion Burger Day Festival attracts some 25,000 attendees to feast on a super-sized burger—250 pounds of beef, 150 pounds of onions, and 350 pounds of bun, cooked on a 12-foot convection oven and 10-foot grill in the middle of El Reno.

The annual feat is an homage to onion burgers, an Oklahoma specialty originated in the Oklahoma City exurb in the 1920s. That's when Ross Davis, then-owner of the bygone Hamburger Inn, improvised out of Depression-era necessity to stretch his

---

Cooked by volunteers, the world's largest onion burger is cut into whopping portions with coffee cans and handed out to hungry festivalgoers for free. More modestly sized onion burgers are also available from other vendors and eateries.

Courtesy of Lori Duckworth/Oklahoma Tourism

money and create a product that was hearty and cheap. He began layering thin beef patties with heaps of slivered onions to make them look bulkier. Smashed and seared on the griddle, the onions caramelize and press into the patties.

El Reno's location on Route 66 helped maintain a stream of hungry passersby. Although Hamburger Inn is no more, its success inspired El Reno businesses to keep the tradition alive: Robert's Grill opened in the 1920s, followed by Johnnie's Grill in the '40s and Sid's Diner in the '80s. All three are still as popular as ever, featuring the humble onion burger, and the fragrant sizzle of onions searing on the griddle.

What started as a preservation tactic evolved into a beefy cottage industry in an otherwise sleepy Route 66 town, paving the way for the Fried Onion Burger Day Festival in 1989. It's the busiest day of the year in El Reno, when travelers come to eat, play games, listen to music, check out the vintage car show, and partake in the consumption of the world's largest onion burger. Today, the Oklahoma onion burger has inspired iterations throughout the state, at local mini chains like Tucker's Onion Burgers and the Garage, but it's these timeworn institutions—and this festival—that have come to exemplify America's most underrated regional burger.

ROBERT'S GRILL

WHAT: The oldest onion burger joint in Oklahoma

WHERE: 300 S Bickford Ave., El Reno

COST: Prices vary

PRO TIP: The move is to order a chili-slathered Coney dog—as an "appetizer"—while you wait for your burgers to cook.

Sid's Diner. Courtesy of Lori Duckworth/Oklahoma Tourism

95% OF AN APACHE ICON'S GRAVE

How did a US president wind up with Geronimo's skull?

Born in the 1820s, under the Apache name Goyahkla (One Who Yawns), Geronimo earned his name from Mexican soldiers, who tangled with the tenacious warrior in combat. A staunch defender of his people, Geronimo fought in raids in Mexico and the the US. Those raids forced government negotiations, though Apache tribes were confined to reservations, prompting Geronimo to escape and continue combat before surrendering to General Nelson A. Miles in 1886.

A prisoner of war, Geronimo was sentenced to labor at Fort Pickens in Florida before ending up at Fort Sill in southern Oklahoma for the remainder of his years. Although a prisoner, his reputation warmed, and he appeared at events like the 1901 Pan-American Exposition in Buffalo, and President Theodore Roosevelt's inauguration parade in 1905. Ultimately, his reputation wasn't enough to get the federal government to release him, and he died at Fort Sill in 1909. He was buried at the base's Apache Cemetery, under a pyramid-shaped gravestone adorned with an eagle. But there's one piece missing.

Nine years after Geronimo's death, Fort Sill members from a Yale University fraternity called the Order of Skull and Bones dug up the grave, stole his skull, and took it to Yale. One such member was Prescott Bush, father of President George H. W. Bush. The fraternity allegedly stashed the skull at their clubhouse,

---

The several hundred other Apache graves at the Fort Sill cemetery include Geronimo's wife, Zi-yeh, and daughter Eva Geronimo Godeley.

Courtesy of Lori Duckworth/Oklahoma Tourism

APACHE CEMETERY

WHAT: The final resting place of one of the most famous Native American warriors

WHERE: Elgin Rd. and Dodge Hill Rd., Fort Sill

COST: Free

PRO TIP: Since Geronimo's grave is on the Fort Sill army base, visitors need either an approved military ID or permission from the Fort Sill Visitor Center.

the Skull and Bones Tomb. While the myth has never been confirmed, author Marc Wortman uncovered a letter at Yale's Sterling Library, from one frat member to another, that contained damning evidence: "The skull of the worthy Geronimo the Terrible exhumed from its tomb at Fort Sill by your club and the Knight Haffner is now safe inside the Tomb, together with his well-worn femurs, bit, and saddle horn."

Geronimo's descendants have filed lawsuits, calling for the return of the skull and the re-interment of Geronimo's remains on Apache land. For now, though, one of the bravest Apache leaders remains buried at Fort Sill, while the whereabouts of his skull remain a macabre mystery.

Courtesy of Oklahoma Historical Society

A STANDOUT MOMENT IN THE SIT-IN MOVEMENT

Did the civil rights movement actually start in Oklahoma City?

In 1958, two years before the officially recognized start of the sit-in movement in North Carolina, a black school teacher named Clara Luper took a bold stance—by sitting down.

A history teacher at Dunjee High School, Luper traveled to New York City in 1957 with students to perform a play she wrote, called *Brother President: The Story of Dr. Martin Luther King.* She became inspired by non-violent activism, especially sit-ins, as a means of protesting segregation. Upon her return, she sought to enact a similar strategy in Oklahoma, starting with a peaceful protest at the Katz Drugstore lunch counter, with members from the NAACP Youth Council. The idea was simple: rally at Luper's house, proceed to the drugstore for lunch, and refuse to budge when denied service for being black. They weren't served, but two days later, Katz's corporate management desegregated its lunch counters in three states, including Oklahoma.

It was among America's first sit-ins, leading to like-minded protests, marches, and boycotts across the country. Although

Courtesy of Oklahoma Historical Society

Luper was arrested 26 times, her efforts paved the way for the Oklahoma City Council to enact an ordinance ending racial discrimination before the federal Civil Rights Act in 1964. After her Katz sit-in, Luper helped integrate hundreds of businesses throughout the state, as well as partake in marches across the country, including the 1963 March on Washington, where Dr. King gave his "I Have a Dream" speech, and the Selma-to-Montgomery march in 1965, when her leg was cut on "Bloody Sunday."

Among Luper's influences, one of her students became the first black chief of police in Oklahoma City, and she was inducted into the Oklahoma Hall of Fame. A $25 million Clara Luper Civil Rights Center is in the works at the Freedom Center of Oklahoma City, to include a five-acre campus with sit-in exhibitions, a café, a welcome center, events spaces, and a community gathering place.

Courtesy of Oklahoma Historical Society

FREEDOM CENTER OF OKLAHOMA CITY

WHAT: The nonprofit hub of the civil rights movement in Oklahoma, and future home of the Clara Luper Civil Rights Center

WHERE: 2609 N Martin Luther King Ave., Oklahoma City

COST: Free

PRO TIP: A $3.6 million bronze monument to the Clara Luper Sit-In is being installed in downtown Oklahoma City where the Katz Drugstore once stood.

In 2023, Senate Bill 509 was passed to implement a statewide Civil Rights Trail, to start at Standing Bear Park in Ponca City and linking 13 of Oklahoma's remaining all-black towns, before ending at the Clara Luper Civil Rights Center.

HOW A STAR ARCHITECT FADED INTO A FOOTNOTE

Why did one of the country's most whimsical designers fade into anonymity?

While architects like Louis Sullivan and Frank Lloyd Wright are household names, one singular designer has flown under the radar. Bruce Goff, born in 1904 in Kansas, moved to Tulsa at an early age and developed a love for architecture, working at the age of 12 for Rush, Endicott and Rush architecture firm.

Like his mentor Wright, Goff employed an admiration for organic aesthetic, pulling inspiration from nature and incorporating varied textures and natural light. He was also whimsical, repurposing everything from ashtrays to cake pans for decor, even tinkering with carpeted roofs and indoor water gardens. Some of his structures, many in and around Tulsa, looked more like *The Jetsons* than Oklahoma, like the Bavinger House in Norman. Prior to its demolition in 2016, the house was a beacon of innovation—anchored around a 96-foot-tall sandstone beacon that

BOSTON AVENUE UNITED METHODIST CHURCH

WHAT: An Art Deco icon in an Art Deco epicenter

WHERE: 1301 S Boston Ave., Tulsa

COST: Free

PRO TIP: Guided tours are available every Sunday at 12:15 p.m., and self-guided tours are available throughout the week.

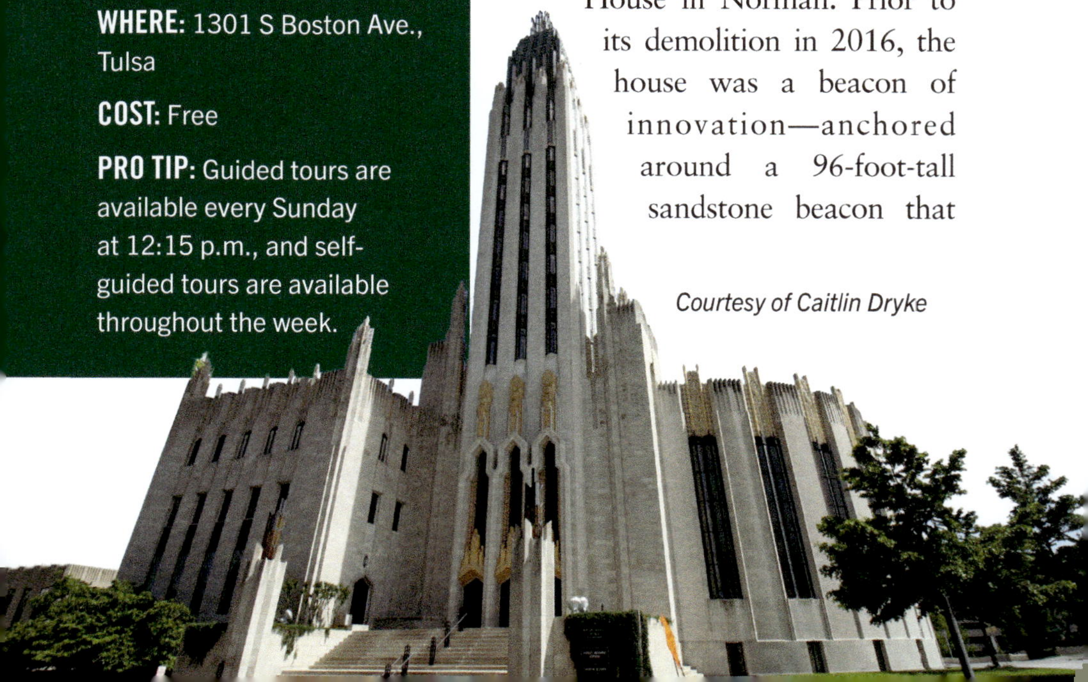

Courtesy of Caitlin Dryke

jutted through the middle. Another masterpiece is the 255-foot-tall Boston Avenue United Methodist Church. Completed in 1929, it's considered one of the foremost examples of ecclesiastical Art Deco architecture in the country.

But just like Bavinger House, Goff's legacy has comparatively been lost to time. Much of that has been chalked up to homophobia, as Goff was a closeted gay man. After teaching at the College of Architecture at the University of Oklahoma, he resigned in 1955 after getting arrested for allegedly "endangering the morals of a minor." This came after a university colleague, Henry Kamphoefner, resigned over distaste for Goff's sexual orientation.

Courtesy of Tulsa Club Hotel

Retreating from public life, Goff lived out the rest of his days in quiet. His final work, the Japanese Pavilion at the Los Angeles County Museum of Art, was completed after his death in 1982, and while many of his peers' works have been preserved, many of Goff's remaining structures are in disrepair, and the Shin'enKan home in Bartlesville burned down.

Fans have rallied around him anew. Goff Fest is a queer-centric festival in Tulsa that leans into the campiness of the architect and features events like a Beaux Arts ball, where people dress up like Goff's buildings.

The city of Tulsa has declared June 8 to be Bruce Goff Day, which just so happens to be Frank Lloyd Wright's birthday.

THE CENTER OF THE UNIVERSE

Is the urban acoustic phenomenon really the middle of all existence?

In the middle of Tulsa's urban core, sandwiched between the Arts District and the Blue Dome District, a pedestrian bridge contains a nondescript brick pathway, culminating in a small circle. To the casual passerby, it's hardly noticeable, but for those on the lookout, it's the epicenter of creation. Or some architectural acoustic trickery, depending on whom you ask—or how loudly you speak while standing in the middle of said circle.

The Center of the Universe—which emerged in its brick form in 1983—gets its lofty moniker from the sonic vortex it causes. When standing in the middle of the brick circle, anyone who speaks hears their voice loudly reverberate back at them, while those outside the circle hear a hushed sound, if anything. Some visitors report being able to shout while standing in the circle, and no one around, even

BOSTON AVENUE PEDESTRIAN BRIDGE

WHAT: A mysterious urban vortex in the middle of downtown Tulsa

WHERE: 1 S Boston Ave., Tulsa

COST: Free

PRO TIP: This is best experienced with a friend. Take turns standing in the middle of the brick circle to experience the echo chamber.

Be sure to check out the adjoining art installation, *Artificial Cloud*, a 60-foot sculpture by Chiricahua Apache artist Bob Haozous that surrounds a soaring cloud with planes and passengers.

from just a few feet away, can hear. The vortex is almost certainly a natural distortion caused by sound bouncing off nearby circular walls, but studies have yet to reveal an agreed-upon consensus.

Over the years, the Center of the Universe has become a quirky, in-the-know tourist attraction, as well as a place for irreverent photos and even marriage proposals. But despite its claim as the center of existence, it's largely been neglected and left in disrepair. Thus, a new initiative, Reimagining the Center of the Universe, is a project with Downtown Tulsa Partnership and the City of Tulsa to capitalize on this unique phenomenon. This includes beautifying the area and encouraging walkability via shaded areas and green space, while landscape designers are working with acoustics specialists to ensure the vortex itself isn't altered.

A mysterious vortex in downtown Tulsa may or may not be the center of the universe. Courtesy of Lori Duckworth/Oklahoma Tourism

A CASTLE FIT FOR A GOVERNOR

How did Oklahoma's medieval-looking Tucker Tower go from secret summer retreat to nature center?

Built in the 1930s and completed two years after Lake Murray became Oklahoma's first state park, the 65-foot Tucker Tower stands on land overlooking Lake Murray that was once home to the Kichai tribe of the Wichita Indians, before being used as a hideaway for outlaws. After Oklahoma joined the Union and the rapscallions departed, the state's most eccentric governor put his own stamp on it. William H. "Alfalfa Bill" Murray, a Texas-born farmer-turned-lawyer, was elected to Congress in 1914. After a decade abroad in Bolivia, Murray returned to Oklahoma amidst the throes of the Great Depression and was elected Democratic governor in 1930.

Courtesy of Keli Clark/Oklahoma Tourism

An anti-establishment politician who prided himself on being "of the people," Murray shunned New Deal legislation in favor of boosting Oklahoma's own economy. Part of this was established with the construction of Tucker Tower, initially designed as a secret—and decidedly decadent—summer retreat for himself and subsequent governors.

The tower was inspired by photos of European castles captured by World War I veteran Fred Tucker, constructed by Works Progress Administration crews using limestone from the lake's basin. The tower was never used by Murray, or any governor, but lay dormant until it was repurposed into a natural history and geological museum in 1950. Open to the public, the preserved-in-time structure offers a glimpse into what life was like in the '30s, as well as what could have been for Oklahoma's powerful elite. The 360-degree views from the top offer a panorama of the shimmering lake, its surrounding forests, the Arbuckle Mountains, and Texas.

TUCKER TOWER

WHAT: A would-be retreat for governors transformed into a sky-scraping nature center

WHERE: 18407 Scenic Hwy. 77, Ardmore

COST: Fee to park

PRO TIP: For a governor-worthy experience, treat yourself to a stay at one of the park's 56 historical cabins, built in the 1930s by the Civilian Conservation Corps.

Even more bizarre is the fact that the tower's museum contains the Lake Murray Meteorite. Estimated to weigh about 2,000 pounds when it struck present-day Lake Murray some 90 million years ago, it's the largest of its kind found in Oklahoma, and fifth largest in the world.

At 12,500 acres, Lake Murray is Oklahoma's first—and still largest—state park, complete with 10 campgrounds, 30 miles of trails, and 150 miles of shoreline.

THE PALACE THAT OIL BUILT

How did an Italian palazzo come to be the epicenter of drama in rural Oklahoma?

From rags to riches, oil money is a tale as old as time in Oklahoma. Literally overnight, prospectors could strike oil at random—and strike it rich. Such is the legacy of Ernest Whitworth "E. W." Marland, a Pittsburgh native who flocked westward in hopes of discovering oil of his own. Not only did he succeed, but at one point, the overnight tycoon owned one-tenth of the world's oil reserves.

After drilling oil in Ponca City, Marland used his wealth—a personal net worth of $30 million at the time—to construct a lavish mansion in 1928, clocking in at $5.5 million and 43,000 square feet, inspired by Italian palazzos. The ensuing years of fame and infamy were like something off a soap opera, including the death of E. W.'s first wife, Mary Virginia; the marriage to his adopted daughter Lydie; and the overthrow of his oil empire by J. P. Morgan Jr.

The lore, sordid and all, is on decadent display at the Marland Mansion and Estate, a colossal property in Ponca City inspired by the Davanzati Palace in Florence, Italy. The home contains four floors, 55 rooms, a Prohibition-era tunnel used to discreetly transport liquor into a subterranean "whiskey room," and a sprawling ground-level dining

MARLAND MANSION AND ESTATE

WHAT: A prairie palazzo and an icon of wealth and infamy in Oklahoma oil country

WHERE: 901 Monument Rd., Ponca City

COST: Small fee for entry, free for kids under 6

PRO TIP: Marland's first Ponca City home, his Grand Home, is located nearby and contains myriad artifacts and the first indoor swimming pool in Oklahoma.

room specifically designed for morning meals before fox hunts. Decked out with Waterford crystal chandeliers, gilded ceilings, hand-carved angels, an in-ground swimming pool the size of two Olympic-sized pools combined, and one of the first electric saunas in the country, Marland spared no expense for his dream home, despite the fact that he lived in it for less than two years. Exploring the mansion and its grounds offers a glimpse at the glory that could come with Oklahoma oil money, as well as the unexpected costs that come with it.

Photos courtesy of Lori Duckworth/Oklahoma Tourism

When Marland fell on hard financial times, he did what all of us would do: become the 10th governor of Oklahoma.

STOP AND SMELL THE ROSE ROCKS

What is the one thing that only Oklahoma and Morocco have in common?

250 million years ago, tropical seas covered the present-day Great Plains. Oklahoma, now a landscape of grasslands and oil-rich ranches, was once a shallow bay. Amidst it all, oceanic barite and sand conjoined during the Permian Period, crystalizing around grains of quartz as the sea ebbed, leaving behind a reddish-brown stone with peculiarly shaped petals that seem to blossom. The barite rosette, commonly known as the rose rock, was born.

Over millions of years, as the continents shifted and North America settled into its shape, the rose rocks remained. Today, these relics of the Permian past can be found scattered across a particular band in central Oklahoma, largely in and around the town of Noble, and while similar—albeit far smaller—bands have been discovered in Kansas and California, the only other place on Earth where they're as abundant as Oklahoma is . . . Morocco.

Like floral fossils, most rose rocks range from the size of a pea to roughly four inches around, while clusters can clock in at a staggering 1,000 pounds. In towns like Noble, Norman,

Courtesy of Oklahoma Historical Society

Creations made from rose rocks were the contribution of Norman's Joe Stine to the array of Oklahoma artists' works lining the State Capitol rotunda. Courtesy of Oklahoma Historical Society

and Pauls Valley, they can be found in the dirt and strewn along lakeshores, and they're such a regional novelty that they've inspired a veritable cottage industry of tourism, geology, and art. Before its closure in 2019, the Timberlake Rose Rock Museum featured works of rose rock art and bountiful specimens of the stone—some of which have since been donated to Noble City Hall. In 1968, Governor Dewey Bartlett declared it the state rock, and in 1984, Governor George Nigh named Noble the rose rock capital of the world.

Today, Noble retains that crown proudly. In addition to rose rock riches in the soil, the town features the world's largest collection of rose rocks at the Tree Wizard Workshop and Gallery, and the chamber of commerce features a Rose Rock Musical Festival every May.

Once upon a time, a Cherokee myth held that rose rocks were formed from the tears of women—and the blood of men—shed during the Trail of Tears from Georgia to Oklahoma.

TREE WIZARD WORKSHOP AND GALLERY

WHAT: An eclectic art gallery contains an exhibit dedicated to rose rocks.

WHERE: 201 N Main St., Noble

COST: Free to visit

PRO TIP: The gallery contains an original letter from Mary Joe Kuhlman, who campaigned for the rose rock to become Oklahoma's state rock.

THE SMILE SEEN AROUND THE WORLD

How did a cartoon Eskimo become a symbol of Oklahoma bar culture?

The second most collectible T-shirt in the world, behind Hard Rock Cafe, doesn't belong to a big brand or a conglomerate but rather an Eskimo-themed sports bar in Stillwater. A self-described "Jumpin' Little Juke Joint Since 1975," Eskimo Joe's is a place of curious history and success, a place with an unexpected mascot seen all over the world, and perhaps even more notably, a place of cheese fries.

ESKIMO JOE'S

WHAT: What originated as a college bar boomed into an Oklahoma legend thanks to a smiling Eskimo.

WHERE: 501 W Elm Ave., Stillwater

COST: Menu prices vary.

PRO TIP: The restaurant can get packed, so skip the line by heading upstairs for open seating at one of the bars.

Located steps from Oklahoma State University, Eskimo Joe's emerged in 1975 as a humble passion project for childhood friends Steve File and Stan Clark. The duo found a two-story downtown building for rent, came up with a quirky name, and used a magic marker illustration from a local art student to create what would become an indelible symbol for Stillwater and the entire state. On opening day, 72 T-shirts were available for sale behind the bar, each emblazoned with a widely grinning Eskimo and his husky, Buffy. They sold out in a week, generating such demand that the bar eventually added a massive retail store.

Once the drinking age was raised to 21 in 1984, Eskimo Joe's evolved into a full-service restaurant, garnering particular fanfare—including from President George H. W. Bush—for its plethora of cheese fries. But no menu item would ever hold a candle to the merch, for a brand so popular that its annual anniversary celebrations have attracted block party crowds of 65,000, rivaling OSU football games. Nowadays, the "smile seen around the world" is one of an Oklahoma Eskimo beaming with hometown pride.

Eskimo Joe's "wall of fame" displays photos of customers wearing T-shirts all over the world, from the Eiffel Tower to Stonehenge.

Photos courtesy of Eskimo Joe's

THE MINI MOSQUE THAT SHAPED A CITY

What do Route 66 and Istanbul have in common?

The Blue Dome District in downtown Tulsa reigns as one of the foremost neighborhoods in the state for nightlife, dining, shopping, festivals, and street art. And it's all thanks to a 24-hour service station designed like a Turkish landmark. A century ago, the titular Blue Dome was a gas station on Route 66, at the intersection of Second and Elgin. But it wasn't just any gas station—it was a surprisingly lavish gas station modeled after the Hagia Sophia, the iconic mosque in Istanbul.

The aptly dubbed Blue Dome, named for its striking cerulean roof over a gilded Art Deco facade, arose during Tulsa's oil-boom heyday in the 1920s. Initially known as the White Star Service Station and crafted in a rounded shape by architects Lawrence Blue and Fred L. Knoblock, it opened in 1925 to serve passersby on their way across the under-construction Route 66. Distinct among gas stations, past or present, the rotund architectural marvel was Tulsa's first 24-hour filling station—manned by a service attendant who lived on-site inside the dome.

When Route 66 officially opened in 1926, the Blue Dome was ready to dazzle. Along with a slew of other roadside attractions and oddities, the White Star Service Station quickly earned its fair share of fanfare from road-trippers who stopped to fill up and marvel at its mystifying motif. Although a fraction of the real mosque's size, the station's distinct shape and its sky-blue corona made it a marquee attraction on America's Mother Road.

Thanks to its namesake dome, the Blue Dome District was listed on the National Register of Historic Places in 2011.

As was the fate of so many other roadside stopovers on Route 66, the gas station closed in the '50s, but its legacy remained. For decades, until 1999, the dome operated as Veterans Bar. It also housed an antiques shop. Today, it shares ownership with the adjoining Irish pub, Arnie's Bar. It's no longer open to the public, but the Blue Dome has left an indelible mark on Tulsa's architectural landscape, the original lore of Route 66, and the patchwork of neighborhood amenities and attractions that now calls the Blue Dome District home.

THE BLUE DOME

WHAT: A dome-shaped former gas station is now the namesake star of one of Tulsa's buzziest neighborhoods.

WHERE: 202 S Elgin Ave., Tulsa

COST: Free

PRO TIP: The Blue Dome is best viewed from adjacent Arnie's Bar, a longstanding Irish pub (since 1956) that's particularly known for its extravagant St. Patrick's Day parties.

Courtesy of Lisha Newman/Oklahoma Tourism

THE BERMUDA TRIANGLE OF THE PLAINS

What caused Spanish conquistadors to disappear in the panhandle?

BEAVER DUNES PARK

WHAT: A state park known for sand dunes is also nicknamed the Oklahoma Bermuda Triangle.

WHERE: US-270, Beaver

COST: Small fee to visit the dunes

PRO TIP: For those who don't disappear, the Big Sandy picnic area in the park is a haven for sand volleyball, horseshoe pits, and the mile-long Pioneer Interpretive Trail.

In a quiet stretch of the Oklahoma panhandle, the small town of Beaver is an innocuous community, home to Beaver High School, Beaver River, Beaver Lake, and beaver mascots. Then there's Beaver Dunes Park, a sandy landscape mostly visited by off-roaders and ATVs. The 520-acre park is an oasis for hiking, fishing, and camping, but sinister secrets lurk beneath the sand.

Since the 1500s, centuries before Oklahoma even tinkered with the idea of statehood, people have gone mysteriously missing in those dunes—so much so that Beaver Dunes Park is more infamously known as Shaman's Portal, No Man's Land, or the Oklahoma Bermuda Triangle. In the 16th century, the region was a lawless melee of Spanish conquistadors and Indigenous tribes, with some of the earliest exploration happening under the direction of

"Green lightning" is the scientific term assigned to what allegedly happened to Coronado's men—an atmospheric occurrence that turns lightning a greenish tint.

Francisco Vázquez de Coronado. As legend has it, he discovered the dunes in 1541—much to the dismay of three of his men, who disappeared inexplicably after following floating green lights. Coronado detailed the occurrence in journals, describing seeing his men vanish in flashes of green light as "the work of the devil."

In the ensuing centuries, similar disappearances have been cited enough to earn the dunes nicknames like Shaman's Portal, coined by Native tribes who tried to warn Coronado about its dangers. Numerous attempts to explain the phenomenon include the maybe-fact that the land is an ancient Native American burial ground, or that it was the site of a UFO crash, à la Roswell. The latter would explain visitor reports of seeing the US military digging in the sand in the middle of the night.

Whatever happens in the deserted dunes, be it ancient hauntings or an alien cover-up, it remains to be seen what actually befell Coronado's men—and countless others who have reported odd sightings and disappearances in this Bermuda Triangle of the Great Plains.

Courtesy of Oklahoma Tourism

THE DUST BOWL FOREST

Why were 20,000 red cedars planted in perfect rows six feet apart in every direction?

A massive, years-long drought in the 1930s turned the Great Plains into a veritable Great Desert, devoid of crops and grappling for survival. The Dust Bowl, which lingered from 1930 until 1936, saw the demise of countless farm animals, the closure of myriad businesses, and the departure of numerous families, fleeing states like Oklahoma and Kansas in search of greener pastures. Without enough water for grass or crops, and with fierce dust storms that inhibited growth, the region was starved and parched for more than half a decade.

To counter the effects of said dust storms and to ward off potentially similar weather phenomena in the future, the government intervened. They did so by planting 20,000 red cedars, a non-native species selected for its ability to grow upward in close, narrow proximity. Planted exactly six feet apart in every direction across 16 acres, the tall trees were implemented as a shield from the wind. But as with any forest like this, one of unnatural symmetry contrived—and subsequently abandoned—by the federal government, creepy lore proved inevitable.

PARALLEL FOREST

WHAT: A government-planted forest designed to counter the effects of the Dust Bowl

WHERE: Meers Rd., Lawton

COST: Free

PRO TIP: Head up Meers Road and wait in the worthwhile line for a burger at the iconic Meers Store and Restaurant.

Located on the eastern edge of the Wichita Mountains Wildlife Refuge, the otherwise nondescript and dark forest is unlike anything around it. Within these 16 unmarked acres, where any semblances of trail blend together as one homogenous labyrinth, the soaring cedars block out not just the wind but also the sunlight. It is eerily quiet and perpetually shaded, and visitors have reported not only getting lost but also

Courtesy of Matt Kirouac

ghostly happenings, like the sound of ancient drums reverberating through the forest, floating orbs, and out-of-body whispers.

Other claims state that the forest was planted by the government as lumber for future park projects, but whatever the reason, its defiant remains as a dark and imposing grove make it a mystical stopover for those drawn to the macabre.

If you can find it, a circle of stones is located toward the back of the forest, said to be used as some sort of altar for witchcraft or satanic rituals.

A HONKY-TONK WITH HISTORY

Why did a rock star punch a hole in the wall at the "Carnegie Hall of Western Swing"?

A progenitor of western swing music, Cain's Ballroom has a long legacy as one of the most enduring music venues in the nation. Built as a garage for Tulsa businessman Tate Brady in 1924, it was transformed into a ballroom, Cain's Dance Academy, in 1930.

The venue's first claim to fame was Bob Wills, a Texan fiddler who became known as the king of western swing and has since been inducted into the Country Music Hall of Fame. In 1933, Wills banded together with musicians from Texas's Light Crust Doughboys to form a band of their own: Bob Wills and His Texas Playboys. Despite its Lone Star moniker, the group—which became seminal in the development of the western swing genre—were inextricably tied to Tulsa's concert hall.

The group frequented Cain's to play for their radio show and became so synonymous with the venue that it earned the nickname the "Home of Bob Wills." Shortly after Wills's death in 1975, it rebranded as Cain's Ballroom, going on to host some of the biggest names in rock, country, and swing, such as Jack White, Leon Russell, U2, the Police, and Van Halen. The most infamous band to perform was the Sex Pistols. While on the band's only American tour, bassist Sid Vicious became agitated in the green room and punched a hole through the wall. Turning lemons into lemonade, the ballroom transformed the

Courtesy of Lori Duckworth/Oklahoma Tourism

Courtesy of Kevin Pyle

green room into its main office, framed the hole in the wall, and even sells merchandise—like buttons—emblazoned with images of the punch.

Now listed on the National Register of Historic Places, the lofty dance hall's preserved-in-time aesthetic, complete with gold-embroidered drapes that say "Cain's: Home of Bob Wills," make it a timeless landmark. And as an icon of Tulsa's Art District, it's helped inspire the addition of nearby attractions like the Woody Guthrie Center and the Bob Dylan Center.

CAIN'S BALLROOM

WHAT: A century-old garage now stands as one of Oklahoma's most storied music venues.

WHERE: 423 N Main St., Tulsa

COST: Ticket prices vary

PRO TIP: Available during shows, Cain's Kitchen serves barbecue-centric fare like ribs, Fritos pie, and pulled pork nachos.

With nicknames like the "Carnegie Hall of Western Swing" and "Blue Collar Palace," the iconic dance hall still features a spring-loaded maple floor illuminated by a four-foot neon star and disco ball.

THE LOST NATIONAL PARK

Courtesy of Lori Duckworth/Oklahoma Tourism

Why was one of the nation's original national parks demoted?

For centuries, the Arbuckle Mountains in southern Oklahoma were an oasis for Paleo-Indians and Indigenous tribes, like the Chickasaws. Amongst some of the oldest mountains on Earth, Native Americans thrived in the mineral-rich springs, but they weren't the only ones to reap the benefits of those healing waters.

Both the Chickasaw and Choctaw nations sold their land to the federal government in 1902. The latter was intent on surfing the wave of hydrotherapy that had been sweeping the country, and seeking to establish a lucrative wellness resort, the government named it the Sulphur Springs Reservation.

Abundant potable water, rife with nourishing minerals as it trickles down off the Arbuckles, was seen as a panacea for everything from digestive ailments to muscle fatigue. Renamed Platt National Park in 1906, after Senator Orville H. Platt, it marked a significant upgrade during a time when similar recreation areas were being designated, like Yellowstone; Yosemite; and Hot Springs, Arkansas. Platt became the seventh national park in the US and the only one in Oklahoma.

Hydrotherapy was all the rage around the turn of the century, but the key distinction between Hot Springs and Sulphur Springs is temperature: the former is hot (147° F), while the latter is cold (63° F).

Courtesy of Lori Duckworth/Oklahoma Tourism

CHICKASAW NATIONAL RECREATION AREA

WHAT: One of the first national parks is now a recreation area for swimming and hiking.

WHERE: 901 W 1st St., Sulphur

COST: Free

PRO TIP: Swimming remains the most popular pastime at the park, with accessible Rock Creek, Veterans Lake, Lake of the Arbuckles, and Travertine Creek west of Little Niagara.

It was the smallest national park but one of the most visited, thanks to its proximity to populated areas, its mythical waters, and its recreational opportunities. Beyond drinking the water, visitors swam in the creeks and lakes, earning the park the nickname "The Playground of the Southwest."

The Civilian Conservation Corps constructed waterfalls in Travertine Creek and dammed up Lake of the Arbuckles, providing a larger body of water for fishing and boating. Considering the park's small scope, and its focus more on recreation than conservation, the federal government sought to turn the park back over to the state. Meanwhile, Oklahomans—and the Chickasaw Nation—fought to maintain its pedigree. After attempting to rename it Chickasaw National Park, the park was combined with Arbuckle Recreation Area and rebranded as Chickasaw National Recreation Area in 1976. Still under the purview of the National Park Service, its well-intended demotion reflects its focus on recreation, while upholding a degree of panache—and providing an oasis for Oklahomans past, present, and future.

THE GREATEST CEMETERY ON EARTH

Why are so many circus animals buried in Southeast Oklahoma?

For many "showmen under God's big top," their final resting place is a nondescript cemetery in the southeast Oklahoma town of Hugo. This blink-and-you'll-miss-it patch of pastoral no man's land was, incidentally, a frequent stop for traveling circuses that started wintering here in the 1930s. Its ample space, mild climate, and proximity to numerous major markets and railways made Hugo a convenient oddity—and earned it the nickname "Circus City, USA." It also made it an apt resting place on a more permanent scale.

Many circuses passed through Hugo, but the fixtures were sister brands the Carson & Barnes Circus and the Kelly Miller Circus. The son of the latter's founder, D. R. Miller purchased a section of the local Mount Olivet Cemetery to bury and memorialize him in a place that had become so integral. Dubbed Showmen's Rest, this particular section has evolved into a macabre spectacle of over-the-top memorials and headstones.

These include graves for animal trainers, jugglers, clowns, and trapeze artists, along with Ringmaster John Strong, whose top hat-wearing headstone reads "the man with more friends than Santa Claus." Some graves memorialize those tragically lost, like John Carroll, crushed by one of the elephants he trained, and Ted Svertesky, who died in a train crash. Others are shaped like circus tents, topped with elephant sculptures, or emblazoned with hippos and chimps. There's also a bench memorializing Mud Show Elephant Man, carved with the words, "Have a Seat on Me."

Hugo's circus culture remains today. A drive around the small town reveals circus trailers parked in driveways and makeshift trapeze swings in yards, while three circuses—Carson & Barnes, Kelly Miller, and Culpepper & Merriweather—still use the town as their headquarters. The Endangered Ark Foundation is a nonprofit retirement ranch for circus elephants, home to the second largest herd of Asian elephants in the US.

MOUNT OLIVET CEMETERY

WHAT: Showmen's Rest is the final resting place for performers in Circus City, USA.

WHERE: 1198 S 8th St., Hugo

COST: Free

PRO TIP: Have lunch at Angie's Circus City Diner, for Southern comfort food in a room decorated with antique circus paraphernalia.

Mount Olivet Cemetery is also home to the Bull Rider's Reprieve, a section that features rodeo stars like Lane Frost (gored during a performance) and Freckles Brown.

Courtesy of Lori Duckworth/Oklahoma Tourism

BOK TOWER

WHAT: A downtown skyscraper designed to be half the size of New York's World Trade Center

WHERE: 1 One Williams Center, Tulsa

COST: Free

PRO TIP: Learn more about Tulsa's architecture boom during its heyday as the Oil Capital of the World by touring the tunnels accessed on South Boston Avenue between Second Street and Fifth Street.

A "MINI" WORLD TRADE CENTER

Why is Tulsa's tallest building a replica of the Twin Towers?

Wander around downtown Tulsa and you may experience a sense of architectural déjà vu. In the heart of the city, soaring above the skyline as the tallest building in town and the second tallest in all five plains states (Oklahoma, Kansas, Nebraska, and the Dakotas), the Bank of America (BOK) Tower is a striking—if not unnerving—homage to the Twin Towers in New York City. In fact, at 52 stories and 667 feet, it's half the size of a single Twin Tower, and one quarter the overall footprint of the former World Trade Center.

When you take a step back into history, the architecture makes total sense. The tower was built three years after the completion of New York's World Trade Center, to resemble the source material almost identically. The vision originated from John Williams, oil magnate and CEO of Williams Companies, who wanted to create an illustrious headquarters for his company in Tulsa. Riveted by the grandeur of the Twin Towers, he initially sought to construct four 25-story replicas, but due to spatial constraints in the city, he pared the plan down to one monolithic skyscraper that, while not quite the height of the World Trade Center, would still break records in Oklahoma and reign as the state's tallest until the Devon Tower arose in Oklahoma City in 2011.

To accomplish this dream, Williams tapped Minoru Yamasaki & Associates, the architects who designed the World Trade Center, with the intent of hewing as closely to the original as possible. Despite its abbreviated scope, the tower was designed as an homage, using steel perimeter columns striated by vertical lines to mirror its larger twins in New York. Inside, the tower's bi-level lobby and marble walls also echo that of the World Trade Center.

Initially dubbed the One Williams Center, the tower shares more synergy with New York than just architecture. Keith Bailey, former chief executive officer of Williams Company, visited the World Trade Center on September 10, 2001, one day before their destruction in the deadliest act of domestic terrorism in US history. He met with the same allied company that John Williams toured in 1973 when he was inspired to replicate the building in Tulsa. On the morning of September 11, 2001, traders in the Tulsa tower were on phone calls with financial colleagues in the World Trade Center. Phones in Tulsa rattled from the explosion, and traders remained on the line to relay final goodbyes before lines went dead and the Twin Towers fell.

In addition to marveling at the World Trade Center replica in downtown Tulsa, visitors can stop by the Center Court Food Hall to dine on chicken sandwiches, smoothie bowls, and barbecue.

Courtesy of Visit Tulsa

THE MOTHER OF THE MOTHER ROAD

How did a service station entrepreneur become the queen of Route 66?

Few Route 66 icons can hold a candle to the undisputed matriarch of the Mother Road, Lucille Hamons. That's thanks to Lucille's Service Station, a roadside relic of yesteryear that still reigns in the blink-and-miss-it town of Hydro in western Oklahoma.

Built in 1929 by Carl Ditmore, and one of only two two-story service stations left on Route 66, it was made to meet the demand for passersby embarking on the newly completed thoroughfare. In 1941, Lucille and Carl Hamons took over the service station, and the former ran the business—while living upstairs—for the rest of the century.

During her tenure, Lucille earned a reputation for her friendliness to motorists and her resilience in the face of development. In 1971, the completion of I-40 severely impacted Route 66, redirecting much of her clientele onto bigger and

---

While surrounding towns were still dry, in the wake of Prohibition, Lucille made a name for herself by selling beer from the station's coolers.

Courtesy of Lucille's

Courtesy of Lucille's

faster roads. The construction of numerous gas stations alongside the interstate also reduced the need for service stations like Lucille's. But Lucille remained steadfast, operating the station—mostly as a souvenir shop—until her death on August 18, 2020.

Her resolute hospitality earned her the nickname "The Mother of the Mother Road," and despite the fact that the service station is no longer operational, it remains a bucket list stop for photos. The Bungalow Craftsman-style property, marked by its open bay layout and vintage gas pumps, is preserved to showcase its legacy. In 1992, commemorating the 66th anniversary of Route 66, the Oklahoma Route 66 Association honored Lucille with a special plaque recognizing 51 years in business. In 1997, the same year the business was added to the National Register of Historic Places, she authored her biography, *Lucille: Mother of the Mother Road*. Her plaque hangs on display at the Oklahoma Route 66 Museum in Clinton.

In addition to photo ops, Lucille's inspired the opening of Lucille's Roadhouse, a Route 66-themed eatery in nearby Weatherford that serves Oklahoma eats like chicken-fried steak, corn nuggets, and of course, Mother Road Burgers.

LUCILLE'S ROADHOUSE

WHAT: This Route 66-themed pitstop pays homage to the mother of the Mother Road.

WHERE: 1301 N Airport Rd., Weatherford

COST: Menu prices vary.

PRO TIP: There's a newer Lucille's Roadhouse location in Clinton, near the Oklahoma Route 66 Museum.

BLACK WALL STREET

Why was a deadly attack on Tulsa's black community swept under the rug for a century?

Shortly after Tulsa became the Oil Capital of the World, turning the city into a wellspring of wealth and opportunity, the Greenwood District was an epicenter of black culture and community. Known for its wealthy residents, the neighborhood was so prosperous that it earned the nickname "Black Wall Street." But that all came to a halt in 1921, when a series of destructive events would alter history forever.

It began when Dick Rowland, a black man, was arrested after riding an elevator with a white woman, Sarah Page. Details of what happened—if anything—are vague, but Rowland was arrested for allegedly assaulting her. Enraged by injustice and racism, black residents rallied around the courthouse, leading to combative mob activity from white men. After shots were fired and the black crowds retreated to Greenwood, their home neighborhood was looted and burned. Governor James Robertson declared martial law, and the National Guard charged in to put out fires and arrest any black person they could find. Altogether, more than 6,000 black people were contained at the Convention Hall and Fairgrounds.

By June 2, a day later, Greenwood lay smoldering. The violence had ceased, but 35 blocks were destroyed, 1,256 homes ravaged, and upwards of 300 people killed. It's dismaying, then, that such a deadly racist attack has long been ignored in history books, and a Race Riot Commission wasn't enacted until 2001. In their

GREENWOOD RISING

WHAT: A museum dedicated to the history of Black Wall Street and the Tulsa Race Massacre

WHERE: 23 N Greenwood Ave., Tulsa

COST: Fee for entry

PRO TIP: Greenwood native Terry Baccus offers insightful guided walking tours of the district.

Courtesy of Greenwood Rising, Inc.

findings, however, they revealed what residents of Greenwood already knew: Rowland was likely to be lynched after his arrest, and the authorities were not there to help him. Not a single criminal charge was ever filed against any of the white assailants.

A hundred years later, a reckoning is upon us. Opened in 2021, Greenwood Rising is a nonprofit museum and history center commemorating Black Wall Street, honoring the lives lost during the Tulsa Race Massacre, and seeking accountability for those responsible for this blight in American history. Galleries trace the ingenuity of the black community in Tulsa, the origins of the attacks, and ultimately, "The Journey to Reconciliation."

Pathway to Hope, designed to commemorate the centennial of the Tulsa Race Massacre, is a mural-lined walking route that weaves its way through historic sites in the Greenwood District.

Courtesy of Lori Duckworth/Oklahoma Tourism

THE STOLEN STATE CAPITAL

Courtesy of State Capital Publishing Museum

Why did the state seal move from Guthrie to Oklahoma City?

After Oklahoma became the 46th state in 1907, President Theodore Roosevelt sent a congratulatory message to Oklahoma Indian Territory. That message wasn't sent to Oklahoma City, though, but to the state's original capital in Guthrie.

This was the site of the State Capital Company, founded by Frank Hilton Greer, who arrived during the Land Run of 1889 and settled in Guthrie to turn his printing experience into a newspaper industry. He commissioned architect Joseph Foucart to design an ornate building in downtown Guthrie, completed in 1902, and established it as the headquarters for his newspaper, the *Daily State Capital*. The building never served as the state capitol, but at the time, it was here where President Roosevelt's telegram was read aloud from the second-floor balcony.

While Guthrie served as the territorial capital, that title was moved to Oklahoma City in 1910, thanks partly to Greer's polarizing figure. After statehood, Oklahoma was no longer restricted

OKLAHOMA TERRITORIAL MUSEUM AND CARNEGIE LIBRARY

WHAT: A museum commemorating Oklahoma's original capital in Guthrie

WHERE: 406 E Oklahoma Ave., Guthrie

COST: Fee for entry

PRO TIP: The main floor of Guthrie's Carnegie Library, the oldest existing library of its kind in Oklahoma, is open to the public, while records are available for researchers.

Photos courtesy of State Capital Publishing Museum

by the Oklahoma Enabling Act of 1906, which noted that Guthrie needed to be the capital. The new capital was laid to a vote on June 11, 1910, wherein Oklahoma City beat Guthrie by 50,000 votes. Governor Charles Haskell acted swiftly, moving the state seal from Guthrie before final votes were tallied, and called his secretary on election night to have him move the seal. The next day, the governor signed a proclamation declaring the new capital.

Civic leaders in Guthrie filed suits decrying the move, three years before Guthrie's federally promised tenure was set to expire under the Oklahoma Enabling Act. In 1912, an election saw State Question 40 on the ballot, as to whether the capital should move back to Guthrie. It lost to Oklahoma City with 54 percent of the vote saying no. Preservationists purchased the bankrupt State Capital Company, before deeding it to the Guthrie Chamber of Commerce.

Now the State Capital Publishing Museum, the property tells the story of Guthrie's early role in Oklahoma lore. Nearby, the Oklahoma Territorial Museum and Carnegie Library digs deep into the state's rocky start, and how a governor stole the capital overnight.

Downtown Guthrie is designated as a National Historic Landmark, preserving the vitality of the town's architecture and protecting 1,400 acres of the former capital.

ANCIENT PEAKS

Are the Wichitas the oldest mountains on Earth?

Now home to the Wichita Mountains National Wildlife Refuge, the largest of its kind in the state, the Wichita Mountains encompass more than 59,000 acres of mixed grass prairie, freshwater lakes, and granite mountains in southwestern Oklahoma. One of just two locations in Oklahoma where igneous rock can be found above Earth's surface, the ancient mountains began to form about 525 million years ago, followed by momentous geologic uplift a couple of hundred million years later. Once taller than the Rockies, the present-day range now averages between 400 and 1,000 feet above sea level. Mount Scott, at 2,464 feet, is the highest peak in the range.

Named for the Native American tribe that originally inhabited the region, the mountains aren't just rich with geologic history, but also with lore that ranges from Spanish

---

The tallest point in the range, 2,464-foot Mount Scott has a paved road that visitors can drive up, or park at the bottom and hike or bike up for more of a workout.

Courtesy of Lori Duckworth/Oklahoma Tourism

Courtesy of Lori Duckworth/Oklahoma Tourism

traders and President Theodore Roosevelt to the country's last gold rush. Legend tells of hidden Spanish gold in the mountains, Comanches used them as a refuge from marauders, and in 1905, the Wichita Forest and Game Preserve became the first big-game animal refuge in the country. Nearby, Fort Sill was established by the US Army in 1869 to monitor Native tribes on reserves in the region. Meanwhile, one of the last gold rushes took place here in 1901, when 20,000 miners came looking for that hidden treasure. Today, the range is strewn with remnants of yesteryear—abandoned mining equipment and fossils from the Ordovician Period can be found throughout the Wichitas.

Renamed the Wichita Mountains National Wildlife Refuge in 1936, it's a unique patchwork of flora and fauna, home to roving bison, longhorn, prairie dogs, elk, roadrunners, tarantulas, and more. The mountains are nowhere near as tall as they once were, but the landscape tells a tale as old as time.

WICHITA MOUNTAINS NATIONAL WILDLIFE REFUGE

WHAT: Some of Earth's oldest mountains contain a wealth of history and wildlife.

WHERE: 20539 State Hwy. 115, Cache

COST: Free

PRO TIP: The Bison Loop trail is one of the best routes in the park for spotting wild bison, along with animals like longhorn cattle and tarantulas.

ALLIGATORS ON THE PRAIRIE

Do crocodilians actually live in Oklahoma?

Oklahoma may be where the buffalo roam, but North America's largest mammals aren't the only dinosaur-sized species that rove the state. Although their population pales in comparison to bison, alligators can be found in a small section of southeastern Oklahoma, making them the largest—and most unexpected—apex predators in the state.

Oklahoma is the farthest west and north that alligators—found in only 10 states—live and breed in the wild, and while only about 100 of them reside here (a far cry from the two million of them in Louisiana), they thrive in the marshes of Red Slough Wildlife Management Area. Encompassing 5,814 acres, the refuge includes 2,400 acres of wetlands, 1,600 acres of shrub habitat, 1,100 acres of bottomland hardwood forest, and 300 acres of woodlands. One of the most biologically diverse wetlands in the country, Red Slough is a veritable real-life Jurassic Park—home to alligators, black bears, river otters, beavers, and nutria. It is a haven for bird-watchers, and both bald eagles and golden eagles have been known to soar over the slough.

The American alligator, though, is the star. As the only site in Oklahoma where the crocodilians breed in the wild, their nests can be found throughout the wetlands, and they're most

---

Home to 322 species of birds, Red Slough is equally beloved by bird-watchers, who flock to spot rare Oklahoma species like roseate spoonbills, white ibises, wood storks, and black-bellied whistling ducks.

Courtesy Lori Duckworth/Oklahoma Tourism

likely to be seen during spring. To protect the wildlife, cars are prohibited in the park, but its small size and flat terrain make it easily accessible to hikers. From the North Parking Lot, visitors can walk 1.5 miles along the levee road to Otter Lake, Lotus Lake, observation platforms, and a photo blind.

RED SLOUGH WILDLIFE MANAGEMENT AREA

WHAT: The only wild alligators in Oklahoma dwell in this swampy park in the southeastern part of the state.

WHERE: Black Land Rd., Haworth

COST: Free

PRO TIP: Spring through fall is the prime time to visit, and alligators are most active—and visible—March through October.

Red Slough Wildlife Management Area is co-managed by the US Forest Service, the Natural Resources Conservation Service, and the Oklahoma Department of Wildlife Conservation, all working to restore hydrology and replenish the region's once-robust bottomland hardwood forests. Fostering the park's population of alligators—a protected species—is a key part of that conservation goal.

THE TREE THAT INSPIRED HOPE

How did Oklahoma City's "Survivor Tree" travel around the world?

OKLAHOMA CITY NATIONAL MEMORIAL & MUSEUM

WHAT: The tree that miraculously survived the Oklahoma City bombing stands resolute as a symbol of resilience.

WHERE: 620 N Harvey Ave., Oklahoma City

COST: Free to visit the outdoor memorial; small entry fee for the museum

PRO TIP: Visit during the holidays to see the outdoor memorial grounds beautifully adorned with Christmas decor and lights.

On the morning of April 19, 1995, downtown Oklahoma City became the site of the deadliest act of domestic terrorism in US history. The Oklahoma City bombing saw the destruction of the Alfred P. Murrah Federal Building, by way of a 4,000-pound bomb, just across the street from what has become known as the Survivor Tree. Fully exposed to its explosion, the tree should have been destroyed. Along with 168 people killed, nearly 700 more were injured, nine other nearby buildings were ravaged, 25 more were badly damaged, and 312 reported shattered glass. And yet, the tree stood resolute.

Believed to have been planted in the 1920s, the elm initially rose in a residential backyard, before downtown Oklahoma City developed. As the area shifted to commercial development, the tree was the only one spared when the land was paved into a parking lot. It was spared, once again, in the wake of the explosion, as initial plans called to cut the tree down in search of shrapnel and evidence. But once responders were able to salvage enough evidence in its branches and roots, an arborist

Courtesy of Lori Duckworth/Oklahoma Tourism

came in to revive the tree and begin the recovery process—along with the rest of the city, wounded by tragedy.

The Survivor Tree is a focal point at the Oklahoma City National Memorial & Museum, where the outdoor grounds provide solace and serenity. Beyond the memorial, the impact of that tree can be felt far and wide. In 1996, unsure of the tree's survival potential, officials began collecting seeds to replant elsewhere. In 1997, they were distributed to family members of victims, and subsequent seedlings have been planted all over the country, from the Rutherford B. Hayes Presidential Library and Museums in Ohio to the White House lawn. In 2006, survivors of the bombing attended a ceremony in New York City, when a seedling was planted in Hermon A. MacNeil Park to commemorate those lost in—and those who survived—the attacks on September 11, 2001.

Survivor Tree seedlings can now be ordered online, for anyone—anywhere in the world—who wants to grow their own symbol of resilience.

STONE LION INN

WHAT: A real-life Hill House serves as a spooky bed and breakfast.

WHERE: 1016 W Warner Ave., Guthrie

COST: Prices vary for rooms and murder mystery dinner packages.

PRO TIP: October is the busiest month for murder mysteries, so it's advised to book months in advance.

A HAUNTED MANSION

Is this Oklahoma's spookiest house?

Like something envisioned by Shirley Jackson or Stephen King, the Stone Lion Inn looms large over the historic town of Guthrie. Established in 1907, the same year that Oklahoma became a state and Guthrie was declared the first territorial capital, the Victorian manor is as famed for its architecture as it is infamous for its supposed hauntings.

Formerly the home of the Houghton family, built across 8,000 square feet and four floors, it was the most expensive home in town upon its completion. The Houghton family consisted of 12 children, who lived in the four-story home until the death of Augusta Houghton, who succumbed to whooping cough when a nurse gave her the wrong medicine by mistake. The home became the Smith Funeral Home for a short stint afterward, until a new owner converted it into a B&B.

Courtesy of Lori Duckworth/Oklahoma Tourism

Courtesy of Lori Duckworth/Oklahoma Tourism

Once Becky Luker purchased the home and began renovations in 1986, reports emerged of slamming doors and unexplained footsteps. After her son put his toys away at night, the family would awake in the morning to find them strewn—inexplicably—all over the room. Mr. Houghton, the original patriarch, has been sighted, and guests have noted smelling his tobacco. From the sound of kids jumping on beds to wooden balls rolling across the floor, sightings and disturbances have run the gamut.

Today, Stone Lion Inn is an old-fashioned B&B known for hosting murder mystery dinners. Six guest rooms are on the second floor, while a library and parlor serve as the setting for themed parties downstairs. The mysteries are original stories that weave into the home's haunted past and provide the perfect setting for a spooky outing. Luker still owns the property and writes all the mysteries herself, as she's done since the beginning, when she took out an ad, "How to Plan a Murder," in the *Oklahoma Gazette*. Nowadays, Oklahoma's first B&B is still a blast from the past—and the most legitimate locale for frightful fun.

One of the murder mysteries centers around the real-life death of Elmer McCurdy, who died in a local shootout in 1911 and whose grave lies in Guthrie's Summit View cemetery.

THE SKYSCRAPER THAT LAVA BUILT

Just how tall does Oklahoma get?

In the far-western reaches of the Oklahoma panhandle, the landscape abruptly shifts from shortgrass prairie to rocky mountains. Welcome to Black Mesa, where the Southwest meets the West, and the tallest point in Oklahoma soars above the plains.

30 million years ago, the panhandle was a far cry from the pastoral prairie that dominates today. Volcanoes and magma have long since ebbed, but geologic remnants hearken to the extremities of yesteryear. Near the town of Kenton is where Oklahoma's elevation begins to slope upward, culminating with the highest point in the state, Black Mesa, which clocks in at 4,973 feet. To put that in context with the rest of the state, Oklahoma City's elevation is 1,198 feet, and Tulsa is just over 700 feet. Nearly reaching a mile in height, it's the best place in the state for panoramic views, and nature at its most primitive.

Black Mesa is the focal point of the 1,600-acre park, home to trails and a multitude of animal and plant species. Here, at the easternmost point of the Rocky Mountains, the prairie cedes the spotlight to cacti, juniper, and shrub oak, while golden eagles soar overhead and black bears, bobcats,

Courtesy of Lori Duckworth/Oklahoma Tourism

Courtesy of Lori Duckworth/Oklahoma Tourism

mountain lions, bighorn sheep, and antelope roam. The park's main trail, the Black Mesa Summit Trail, ranks among the toughest in the state. At 8.4 miles roundtrip, it's a strenuous ascent that culminates with a granite summit marker and sweeping views in every direction. It takes about four hours round-trip to complete, and it's advised—no matter the season—to bring ample water, sunscreen, and a light source (like a headlamp).

Camping is allowed within the park, and the area contains some of the darkest night skies not only in Oklahoma, but nationwide. Astronomers come from near and far to gaze at the stars, while August sees the annual Perseid meteor shower put on a celestial show.

BLACK MESA STATE PARK

WHAT: This panhandle state park contains the highest point in Oklahoma.

WHERE: OK-325, Kenton

COST: Free

PRO TIP: Lake Carl Etling, the main water source in the park, is at its highest in the winter and spring, making it ripe for fishing and boating.

The Southern High Plains Initiative is an area organization dedicated to grassland conservation in a precise corner of the country where such terrain teems.

Courtesy of Oklahoma Historical Society

A WHALE ON ROUTE 66

How did the largest animal in the ocean come to symbolize the Mother Road?

BLUE WHALE OF CATOOSA

WHAT: A giant whale is quintessential roadside kitsch on Route 66.

WHERE: 2600 N State Hwy. 66, Catoosa

COST: Free

PRO TIP: A seasonal on-site gift shop sells Blue Whale merchandise, as well as souvenirs made exclusively in Oklahoma.

A massive replica of the largest animal in the sea is not the most obvious sight on Route 66. For one imaginative innovator, though, the Blue Whale of Catoosa was perfect. The whale, located northeast of Tulsa, was conceptualized by Hugh S. Davis, a local zoologist who sought to create something spectacular for his animal-adoring wife, Zelta. Especially fond of whales, she had a collection of figurines that inspired her husband to bestow her with something far grander. By anchoring it in a pond close to their home, he envisioned it as an anniversary present for his wife, as well as a makeshift water park.

Davis's sketches for the whale reached up to 80 feet long and 20 feet high, which he achieved with the help of a friend, Harold Thomas. They welded the metal frame and used hand-

The Blue Whale sits in a pond that was once filled with alligators, as part of Hugh's Nature Acres amusement park.

mixed cement to bind it together. Hugh initially wanted to paint it black and white, like a killer whale, but Zelta suggested a gentler species would be more inviting. After a coat of bright-blue paint over the smiling whale, the project was finished in 1972, complete with porthole-style windows, a wide-open mouth that people could walk into, and a slide into the pond. Not only did it make a splash with Davis's wife and grandchildren, but it did so with passersby. The Blue Whale of Catoosa became an instant Route 66 marquee, and a popular stopover for swimming and picnicking.

The pond was a requisite swimming hole, and the whale a Route 66 cornerstone. In Hugh's sunset years, Zelta decided to close the park as a swimming attraction in 1988. Left exposed to the elements and flanked by "No Trespassing" signs, the whale withered for years before the Catoosa Chamber of Commerce stepped in to raise money and restore it to its glory. Today, swimming is no longer permitted at the Blue Whale, but visitors are welcome to picnic, take photos, and wander around the whale that's come to symbolize America's Mother Road.

Courtesy of Lori Duckworth/Oklahoma Tourism

CONCRETE FOLK ART

What led to the creation of a 90-foot totem pole?

If Oklahoma had its own Statue of Liberty or Golden Gate Bridge, it would be the 90-foot totem pole rising along Route 66 in the northeastern town of Chelsea. The totem is the vision of Nathan Edward "Ed" Galloway, a Missouri native with a lifelong love for sculpting and carving. After a stint in the US Army, he returned to his home state rejuvenated and inspired, and began whittling tree trunks into figurines and animals. This led to teaching woodworking classes until retiring in 1937. His retirement was short-lived, as Galloway immediately began work on the most grandiose project of his life—one that would take 11 years to complete.

While living on the land where Ed Galloway's Totem Pole Park currently resides, he drew inspiration from Native American culture to conceptualize an extravagant homage. Influenced by postcards and *National Geographic* magazines, Galloway constructed the main totem pole—working mostly by himself—using red sandstone, steel, wood, and concrete, all set atop a massive three-dimensional sandstone turtle. The totem is hollow throughout its entire 90-foot, nine-story height, lined with interior murals, nature scenes, and Native American iconography.

For 11 years, Galloway toiled on the totem, often waking at 5 a.m. to continue construction. Upon its completion in 1948, some 28 tons of cement later, the tower featured 200 exterior carvings and four nine-

ED GALLOWAY'S TOTEM POLE PARK

WHAT: The tallest concrete totem pole in the world is a Route 66 must-see.

WHERE: 21310 East Hwy. 28A, Chelsea

COST: Free

PRO TIP: Open year-round from dawn to dusk, the park also contains picnic tables, a gift shop, and a half-mile nature trail.

foot Native Americans toward the top. The colorful concrete skyscraper is now the center of a nine-acre totem park, which includes an Arrowhead Totem, a Birdbath Totem, and a Tree Totem. Altogether, the Totem Pole Park was finished in 1961, one year before Galloway's death. For decades, the park was unmaintained, until the Rogers County Historical Society took over in 1989. In 1999, it was added to the National Register of Historic Places, and has remained a quintessential facet of Route 66 lore.

The Totem Pole Park also contains Galloway's "Fiddle House," containing displays of various hand-carved fiddles and other instruments made by the artist.

Courtesy of Lori Duckworth/Oklahoma Tourism

DEEP-FRIED HISTORY AT OKLAHOMA'S OLDEST BAR

Photos courtesy of Lori Duckworth/Oklahoma Tourism

How did a hand-carved bar from Spain wind up in rural Oklahoma?

Fresh off the Land Run of 1889, and more than a decade before statehood, Eischen's Saloon was born in 1896. Founded by Peter Eischen in the tumbleweed-strewn community of Okarche in central Oklahoma, it marked the first watering hole in the territory—one that reigns today as the oldest in the state.

Eischen's evolved through numerous iterations and survived just as many setbacks. It endured Prohibition by closing for a time before reopening—as Eischen's Bar—in the '30s under Peter's son, Nick, and grandson, Jack. In addition to being the oldest operating bar, the designation is two-fold in that the literal back bar is a work of wooden art, hand-carved in Spain in the 1800s. Nick won the bar as a prize on a hunting trip in the '40s and made it the centerpiece of the bar, until much of the building burned in a fire in 1993. Reopened less than a year later, under Peter's grand-grandson Ed, a portion of the bar remains unscathed, along with the rest of the space bedecked with taxidermy, black-and-white photos, and framed newspaper clippings.

During this time, Eischen's developed a reputation for fried chicken. Using a recipe honed in the '60s by George Eischen, who worked as a butcher at a grocer that once stood next door, chickens are dredged in a secret blend of herbs and spices, then fried for 15 minutes in soybean oil at 330 degrees F. They're the star of the menu, served in a spread on platters with sliced white

Courtesy of Lori Duckworth/Oklahoma Tourism

EISCHEN'S BAR

WHAT: The oldest bar in the state serves Oklahoma's most famed fried chicken.

WHERE: 109 S 2nd St., Okarche

COST: Menu prices vary

PRO TIP: There's often a wait at this perpetually popular bar, so arrive before the dinner rush or ask to sit at the bar by the service station in the expanded dining room.

bread, sweet pickles, dill pickles, and onion slivers.

The fried chicken is so famed that it's single-handedly turned Okarche into a tourist attraction for hungry visitors from far and wide. Recipient of numerous "best fried chicken" honors, the bar has played host to famous visitors like Toby Keith, Dennis Quaid, Garth Brooks, Willie Nelson, Amy Grant, and Lee Majors.

When the neighboring IGA grocery store where George Eischen once worked closed in 2004, the bar took over and expanded, adding tables in a space filled with historic grocery ephemera.

THE SPACE COWBOY OF THE GREAT PLAINS

BUCK ATOM'S COSMIC CURIOS

WHAT: A space-aged Muffler Man looms over a Route 66 gift shop.

WHERE: 1347 E 11th St., Tulsa

COST: Free

PRO TIP: The Mother Road Route 66 Passport book, available for purchase at Buck Atom's, allows travelers to get stamps at attractions along the drive.

How does Buck Atom signal a new era for Muffler Men?

Muffler Men represent a special place in Americana. Super-sized fiberglass structures, mostly built in the '60s and '70s and found in multiple states along Route 66, they're colorful characters clad in all manner of costume and persona, from pirates and pioneers to lumberjacks and cowboys. Or in the case of one modern Muffler Man in Tulsa, a space cowboy beckoning in a new era of Route 66 lore.

Buck Atom is the 21-foot Muffler Man standing outside Buck Atom's Cosmic Curios. Once a '50s gas station, the gift shop represents the same fate that befell many service stations along the Mother Road, when newer highways and rail lines drew traffic away and forced businesses to adjust.

Previously, Buck Atom was a defunct Muffler Man sitting in a junkyard in Calgary, Alberta. In 2018, he was pieced back together by fiberglass artist Mark Cline, who was introduced

---

What was formerly a Route 66-themed Airbnb property, located behind the gift shop, is now home to Buck's Vintage, selling everything from matchbooks to denim shorts.

to Buck Atom's Cosmic Curios owner Mary Beth Babcock. As she explored Route 66 in search of kitschy inspiration, she sought to create a Muffler Man for a new generation, and one entirely unique to Oklahoma.

Rather than lease an existing structure, Babcock commissioned Cline for something special. With Buck Atom, she could illustrate a story and create a character, about a roving Oklahoman cowboy who was taken aboard a spaceship for 66 years. After Route 66 waned in visitorship, Buck decided that the road needed his help, so he landed in front of Babcock's shop—complete with a space visor, cowboy hat, and Route 66 belt buckle. A rocket ship, built by Tulsa artist Chris Wollard, was placed in Buck's hands the day before his unveiling in 2019.

Buck Atom offers a bold new take on a timeworn travel tradition, with a distinct cowboy-clad Oklahoma twist. Inside, the shop is brimming with Oklahoma ephemera, from apparel and toys to art, accessories, postcards, coloring books, magnets, buttons, and much more—many of which are emblazoned with Buck Atom himself.

Courtesy of Lori Duckworth/Oklahoma Tourism

A HOUSE FIT FOR A FLINTSTONE

What's the story behind Tulsa's cave-like house in a former restaurant?

Once upon a time, Tulsans flocked to the Cave Garden Restaurant for chicken in a frills-free space just west of downtown. True to its name, the quirky eatery sported a cave-like facade that looked like *The Flintstones* meets the Shire. With jagged stucco walls, labyrinthine rooms, and a fireplace that once led to a hidden speakeasy, the hillside restaurant was unlike any restaurant in Oklahoma. A century later, the restaurant is long gone, but the Cave House remains one of the most whimsical abodes in the country.

Built in the 1920s, the gnarly building doubled as the perfect hideaway during Prohibition. Tunnels formerly led through the fireplace into a speakeasy carved under the hill, like an actual cave. While the tunnel has since been sealed, the mystique of this singular house still lingers—and in some cases, haunts.

Courtesy of Lori Duckworth/Oklahoma Tourism

After the restaurant closed, the Cave House evolved into a literal home for some time. Past residents are said to still reside here, in the forms of mischievous ghosts who hang clothes by the windows or collect visitors' keys. As folklore holds, a ghostly woman is said to haunt the home, as numerous visitors reported losing their keys and finding them on a hill nearby. An on-site "key tree" dangles with keys left behind by curious passersby.

The current owner, Linda Collier, doesn't reside on-site, but she provides tours, and the property acts as a makeshift museum. Inside, visitors can experience the Cave House's narrow halls, precarious staircase, and antique furniture. Collier keeps the quirky lore alive with her collection of hand-crafted artwork made of sticks and bones, like a "bony pony" and "bonezai" tree. Upstairs, a trap door is filled with pennies, and visitors still come from all over the world to voluntarily add keys to the collection, to "keep the key woman happy."

THE CAVE HOUSE

WHAT: A former restaurant is now the funkiest home in Tulsa.

WHERE: 1623 W Charles Page Blvd., Tulsa

COST: Small fee for entry

PRO TIP: Tours are available by appointment; call 918-378-1952.

Gangster Pretty Boy Floyd was among the regulars at the speakeasy, where customers used passwords for entry and ordered whiskey using code words like "horse liniment" or "coffin varnish."

CIRCLE CINEMA

WHAT: Famous Oklahomans are celebrated at Tulsa's very own Walk of Fame.

WHERE: 10 S Lewis Ave., Tulsa

COST: Free to visit; ticket prices vary

PRO TIP: Circle Cinema Film Fest, held every summer, spotlights made-in-Oklahoma films, documentaries, student shorts, and narrative features.

THE OKLAHOMA WALK OF FAME

What do Brad Pitt, Ron Howard, and Tulsa have in common?

Tulsa may be some 1,400 miles from Los Angeles, but that doesn't stop the city from celebrating its home-grown talent with its own Walk of Fame. Much like the Hollywood Walk of Fame, the Circle Cinema Walk of Fame uses aptly circle-shaped markers to celebrate the vast canon of Oklahoma-born talent.

The Oklahoma Walk of Fame features dozens of famed Oklahomans of stage and screen, from all backgrounds and mediums, commemorated along a sidewalk in front of Tulsa's historic Circle Cinema. While the arthouse theater has been airing films for upwards of a century (since 1928), its Walk of Fame is a newer addition that's taken shape over the past several years, as a way to draw attention to Oklahoma's many talents. The Oklahomans celebrated, to many, are surprising.

Brad Pitt, Ron Howard, James Garner, Alfre Woodard, Tony Randall, Chuck Norris, and Joan Crawford are all

---

With some of the best tax incentives in the nation, and recent blockbusters like *Killers of the Flower Moon* and *Twisters* filming here, Oklahoma has emerged as the next great state for Hollywood productions.

Top: Nightmare on Elm Street *alums Heather Langenkamp and Robert Englund visit the Oklahoma Walk of Fame. Courtesy of Circle Cinema. Bottom: Courtesy of Lori Duckworth/Oklahoma Tourism*

among the honorees with ties to Oklahoma. The through line for induction is that they've all lived in Oklahoma at some point in their lives, and every facet of the entertainment industry is eligible, from actors and directors to singers, writers, and beyond. Similar to the Hollywood Walk of Fame, new dedications are occasionally attended by the stars themselves, or members of their family. The most recent dedications were for filmmakers Crystal Kayiza, Kyle Bell, John Swab, and Mickey Reece, along with actor Jay Ellis.

The idea for the Oklahoma Walk of Fame is credited to the Circle Cinema board of directors, who sought to draw more attention to Oklahoma as an epicenter of entertainment and talent. When they discovered that they could create granite markers in circles, befitting the cinema itself, the idea became fully formed. Today, about 50 circular markers round out the Oklahoma Walk of Fame, with room for more in the future.

LIVING KITCHEN FARM & DAIRY

WHAT: Farm-to-table dining doesn't get any more legit than this fine dining farm.

WHERE: 25198 S 481st W Ave., Depew

COST: Dinner prices vary

PRO TIP: Reservations open two to three months in advance, and they tend to fill up, so watch Living Kitchen's website.

FINE DINING IN THE FOREST

How did a woodland cottage become the best fine dining destination in the state?

Nestled in the woods of Depew, a quiet community along Route 66 in between Tulsa and Oklahoma City, Living Kitchen Farm & Dairy is the unlikeliest locale for a fine dining destination, but diners drive from near and far to break bread—along with several other courses—at a communal table on a screened-in porch.

The hidden restaurant is the vision of partners Lisa Becklund and Linda Ford, the former a chef who initially came to Oklahoma to learn how to farm—and wound up staying. She founded Living Kitchen Farm in 2005 and hosted her first

Courtesy Valerie Wei-Haas of Wei-Haas Creative

Chef Lisa Becklund prepares seasonal tasting menus on her farm in Depew. Courtesy of Valerie Wei-Haas of Wei-Haas Creative

farm dinner at her home in 2006. After Ford joined the farm and moved there to live in 2009, the pair leased the 400-acre property and started hosting intimate dinners at their cabin in the woods.

Using ingredients grown themselves or sourced from nearby farms, Becklund and Ford take farm-to-table dining to another level, using their seasonal dinners as a showcase for their bounty. Hosted spring through fall, each tasting menu is a spree of surprises, consisting of multiple courses of twee bites and hearty, shareable plates. In true forested fashion, many courses are cooked over an open fire, served at a communal table large enough to seat 36. The farm spotlights various themes for its dinners, like 10-course plant-based dinners for early spring, heirloom tomato menus in July, and summer menus inspired by Becklund's Pacific Northwest roots, spotlighting fish and mushrooms.

Although located along Route 66, Living Kitchen remains a secret. About a quarter-mile off the route, the farm is the quintessential hidden gem that's still close to cities and highways. Branching off the sustainable success of Living Kitchen, Becklund and Ford opened full-blown restaurants in nearby Tulsa: FarmBar is an upscale restaurant that utilizes ingredients grown on the farm, while il seme is a downtown Italian venture known for its pastas and esoteric wine list.

For her work at FarmBar, Lisa Becklund has been a semifinalist three times for the James Beard Award for Best Chef: Southwest.

A COBBLESTONE OASIS FOR OUTLAWS

What brought Bonnie and Clyde to rural Oklahoma?

Immediately after statehood, Medicine Park was founded in 1908 by John William Elmer Thomas as the Medicine Park Summer Resort and Health Spa, touted and titled for the supposed medicinal qualities in Medicine Creek flowing through town. By building dams, Thomas helped create Bath Lake for swimming and Lake Gondola for boating. The first, and still only, cobblestone community in Oklahoma, the town also distinguished itself with its cobblestone-lined streets and buildings.

Medicine Park attracted more than just swimmers, though. By the '20s, gangsters and bootleggers began to frequent the community, attracting the likes of Al Capone, Pretty Boy Floyd, and even Bonnie and Clyde. Its remote locale, coupled with its small-town feel, made it a haven for folks on the run. It wasn't all ne'er-do-wells (President Roosevelt and Will Rogers also visited the town), but Medicine Park developed a reputation for ruffians.

The Great Depression took a toll, and along with World War II, Medicine Park's tourism struggled for decades. Once a bastion of riverside Americana, the resort community began to crumble—its permanent population dwindling to a record low of 285. Until 1984, when students from the University of Oklahoma worked with the Association for South Central Oklahoma Governments to begin restoration.

Marked by small, round granite cobblestones, made from stones native to the region, cannonball architecture is the term used for the style distinct to Medicine Park.

By the 21st century, Medicine Park had evolved into the resort community it always purported to be. Gone were the gangsters and smugglers. In were the colorful cottages, bustling businesses, cozy restaurants, and festivals. Bath Lake, which washes right up to the main drag, became a fixture for travelers—its waters as restorative and refreshing as the town's earliest reported medicinal creek.

Today, Medicine Park feels like a town from yesteryear. It's seen as both a bedroom community for the greater region and as one of America's foremost cobblestone communities, set amidst the Wichita Mountains. Businesses have remained for generations, bridges look like the stuff of fairy tales, the cobblestones are back to their rocky glory, and families flock to travel back in time and bask in its waters.

MEDICINE PARK

WHAT: A vintage resort community that serves as an oasis for its soothing waters and cobblestone streets

WHERE: Medicine Park

COST: Free to visit (fee to swim in the lake)

PRO TIP: There are no public changing rooms or restrooms in Medicine Park, so wear your bathing suit under your clothes or change in your car.

Courtesy of Lori Duckworth/Oklahoma Tourism

A GHOSTLY MOUND

Was H. P. Lovecraft inspired by a hill in Oklahoma?

Rising 105 feet above the grasslands of west-central Oklahoma, with a distinct stovepipe-like top, Ghost Mound is an apt name for a place routinely circled by vultures and plagued by decades of murky lore.

Out here, mounds and buttes have long been used as landmarks by westward pioneers en route to California for the gold rush. In 1849, Army captain Randolph Marcy led a military escort from Fort Smith, Arkansas, toward California, mapping what would come to be known as the California Road. Travelers gave names to the landmarks, such as Dead Woman's Mound, Twin Mound, and Ghost Mound.

Over the years, stories emerged about Ghost Mound and the area's inhabitants, like the time a Native American woman jumped off the mound—to her death—while waiting for her lost lover to return. Her footprints are said to be visible atop the mound, and visitors report hearing phantom screams around the summit. Another story tells of two Native American brothers who camped alongside the mound. Their horses mysteriously disappeared in the night, leading one brother to go searching—never to return.

Courtesy of Oklahoma Historical Society

Of all the tales, though, it's the theory that horror icon H. P. Lovecraft wrote—or, fittingly, ghost wrote—about the mound. *The Mound* is a horror novella, set in the Oklahoma town of Binger, that Lovecraft allegedly wrote using a pseudonym, depicting a scientist who visits a haunted mound and stumbles into an underground civilization.

The novella was actually penned by Zealia Bishop, a writing student of Lovecraft's, who conceptualized the idea for *The Mound* while in Oklahoma. After she brought the idea to Lovecraft, he supposedly fleshed out the story and wrote 30,000 words on the mound. Much like every other piece of folklore surrounding the mound, the novella—and the literary icon who may have been inspired by it—is shrouded in mystique.

GHOST MOUND

WHAT: The mythical rocky mound that may have inspired an H. P. Lovecraft horror novella

WHERE: North 2460 and East 1110 in Hydro

COST: Free

PRO TIP: The nearby Hinton Historical Museum contains myriad artifacts from the area's California Road heyday.

Courtesy of Oklahoma Historical Society

Ghosts aren't the only things you may or may not find atop Ghost Mound. Dinosaur tracks, particularly those of Utahraptors, can be seen in the rock.

AMERICA'S MOST TOXIC GHOST TOWN

PICHER

WHAT: This once-thriving mining town was abandoned due to lead poisoning and tornadoes.

WHERE: Picher

COST: Free

PRO TIP: The Dobson Museum, in the nearby town of Miami, spotlights local history aplenty, from Route 66 to the *Oklahoma!* musical.

How did a once-thriving mining town go from boom to bust?

In the northeastern corner of Oklahoma, the town of Picher is a skeleton of its former self. Developed in 1913, when lead and zinc were discovered, it's named for O. S. Picher, of the Picher Lead Company. The mining community once boasted a booming economy and a population—ca. 1920—of nearly 10,000. Today, the population is zero, and Picher holds the notoriety of being America's most toxic ghost town.

Picher was the most important mining field in the region, producing more than $20 billion in ore between 1917 and 1947, accounting for more than half the lead and zinc used by the US during World War I. During its peak, more than 14,000 men mined in the Picher Field.

Photos courtesy of Oklahoma Historical Society

Photos courtesy of Oklahoma Historical Society

Exposure to lead, however, made them susceptible to tuberculosis, silicosis, liver failure, and lung cancer, and even after mining dried up in the '60s, the effects plagued ensuing generations. As water from the mines trickled into nearby Tar Creek, wildlife began to die off, and the Environmental Protection Agency expressed concerns about the town's groundwater.

The population dwindled, and a federal study in 2006 showed that hundreds of buildings were in danger of collapse due to undermining and unstable mine shafts. Senator Jim Inhofe helped offer buyouts for residents, leading to the successful relocation of 200-plus families. If lead poisoning and collapse weren't enough, a deadly F-4 tornado leveled a significant portion of Picher in 2008, killing several and ravaging much of the community. Although some residents clung to their community, Picher ceased as a municipality in 2009. Twenty holdouts remained in 2010. By 2015, there was just one: Gary Linderman, owner of the Ole' Miners Pharmacy. The self-described "last man standing" died that year, leaving Picher a ghost town of none.

Today, visitors aren't permitted to enter any of the buildings, but travelers can drive through, walk around, and catch an eerie glimpse into the past.

The Picher Mining Field Museum, a rare remnant from the town's thriving origins, burned in a fire in 2015.

THE SOONER STATE SASQUATCH

Is Bigfoot hiding in Southeast Oklahoma?

Washington may be the state with the most reported Bigfoot sightings, and California may be home to the Bigfoot Scenic Byway, but here in Oklahoma, the mythical cryptid has made a home for himself in the remote forests and mountains in and around the town of Honobia.

Home to more reported Bigfoot sightings than any other part of the state, Honobia—and the more touristy nearby community of Broken Bow—has made a cottage industry of its Sasquatch lore. The Native Oklahoma Bigfoot Research Organization and the Honobia Bigfoot Organization are two groups dedicated to stoking the legend, archiving reports, and in the case of Honobia, hosting an annual festival and conference. The festival, which also includes seminars for Bigfoot "scholars," operated under new leadership for its 2024 run at Kiamichi Mountains Christian Mission at Christ's 40 Acres. Renamed Bigfoot at the 40 Festival & Conference of Honobia, proceeds were earmarked for summer camp

Photos courtesy of Scott Starr

The Native Oklahoma Bigfoot Research Organization has identified massive Bigfoot tracks all over the state, using plaster to document footprints as large as 18 inches long.

Photo courtesy of MOF

scholarships. In addition to the festival and conference, which takes place every October, the campground plans to build upon the Bigfoot connection with events and programming throughout the year.

Bigfoot sightings in the region, a particularly rural swath of land marked by gnarly mountains, babbling brooks, and dense forest, have been swirling for decades, with some hikers reporting direct encounters, hearing growls, spotting hairy beasts as tall as 12 feet, or stumbling upon 20-inch footprints.

HONOBIA BIGFOOT FESTIVAL

WHAT: Annual fall festival and conference dedicated to Bigfoot lore, with food, entertainment, and vendors

WHERE: 37529 Indian Rte. 144, Honobia

COST: Festival is free (fee for conference)

PRO TIP: The easiest way to visit is to camp, and Christ's 40 Acres operates as a campground with spaces for tents and RVs, plus "dorms" with bunk beds.

Stores, restaurants, and breweries maximize the mythos with merchandise and menu specials, like Bigfoot shot glasses and bottled samples of Bigfoot hair at Janet's Treasure Chest in Hochatown. There's also the Bigfoot Speedway, Bigfoot T-Shirts shop, and Squatch burgers at Mountain Fork Brewery. Tourism doubled in the region over the past few years, in part due to the mountains, lakes, and serenity, but also no doubt for the opportunity to see Bigfoot—and the opportunity to believe.

MODERNIST ARCHITECTURE MEETS TELEVANGELISM

Why has Tulsa's most striking building been abandoned for decades?

ABUNDANT LIFE BUILDING

WHAT: The world headquarters for Oral Roberts Ministries is now an empty concrete block.

WHERE: 1720 S Boulder Ave., Tulsa

COST: Free

PRO TIP: Another striking architectural icon in Tulsa is the Prayer Tower, rising like a 200-foot-tall Space Needle over Oral Roberts University.

In a city populated with Art Deco architecture, the most unusual example is a windowless concrete cube that's sat vacant and abandoned since the '80s. Ironic, considering the name of the long-dormant property is the Abundant Life Building, a seven-story behemoth that looks like it crash-landed from another galaxy.

The building came to "life" in 1958, amidst the modernist architecture boom, as the world headquarters for Oral Roberts Ministries televangelists. Its moniker is chalked to founder Oral Roberts's obsession with preaching ("abundant life" is a nod to a Bible passage), and his goal of creating a contained space and community. Outside, the facade—designed by architect Cecil Stanfield—is a looming concrete block of a building, making up the bulk of a city block, clad with diamond-shaped pieces of marble and gold. In lieu of windows, deemed needless next to dazzling new technologies like air conditioning and fluorescents, the interior was anchored by a TV studio where televangelists could broadcast across the globe.

For years, the Abundant Life Building operated in a shroud of mystery, like some kind of televangelist Wizard of Oz. An epicenter of mail from around the world, millions of dollars' worth of donations passed through those concrete walls.

Roberts vacated the building in the mid-'60s, moving his headquarters to nearby Oral Roberts University, and Abundant Life has been dead ever since. Still striking for its futuristic architecture, some Tulsans have held out hope that Abundant Life may live again, in some new form. Some wish for demolition, due to its deteriorating diamond facade and leaky roof, and many view it as a nuisance (the building has seen numerous nuisance violations over the years, including the death of a trespasser in 2013 after falling down an elevator shaft). Preservation Oklahoma named it one of 2016's most endangered historic places, highlighting its mid-century architecture. No matter which side of the debate you stand on, the Abundant Life Building—even in death—still makes its presence known.

Oral Roberts first made a name for himself at 17, when he miraculously healed his own tuberculosis. This inspired him to begin his own "miracle ministry," with his first public healing service in Enid in 1947.

Courtesy of SoBo District/Tulsa Regional Tourism

A GEODESIC DOME WITH GILDED HISTORY

Why is there an EPCOT-shaped sphere in the middle of Oklahoma City?

Of all the Route 66 kitsch in Oklahoma, nothing is more striking than the Gold Dome. Impossible to miss, for its location in the middle of Oklahoma City and for its singular architecture, it's a geodesic dome that spans a dynamic lifetime of different forms and functions.

Constructed in 1958 as a Citizens State Bank and designed by outside-the-box architect Buckminster Fuller, the dome has passed through many operators over the years, including use as an art gallery, office space, restaurant, and cultural center. At the time of its completion, heralded as a forward-thinking innovation in bank design (and the "bank of tomorrow"), it was only the fifth geodesic dome in the world, preceding even the most famed geodesic dome of all: Walt Disney World's EPCOT. It's also one of the only remaining domes of its kind.

Comprising two stories and distinguished by its anodized aluminum roof and 600-plus individual gilded panels, the

Courtesy of Visit OKC

behemoth leaves quite an impression on passersby and road-trippers. It's been empty for years now, at risk of demolition, but it remains one of the most fiercely guarded architectural treasures among preservationists. In 2002, the National Trust for Historic Preservation listed it as one of the "11 Most Endangered Places" in the country, and the dome's importance has been touted by picketing protesters, bumper stickers, songs, and T-shirts. It's sat vacant since 2015, and it's cycled through a laundry list of buyers with would-be hopes for its geodesic future. Those have included everything from a natural grocery store to, most recently, aspirations for a live music venue.

THE GOLD DOME

WHAT: A former bank reigns as one of the world's last remaining geodesic domes.

WHERE: 1112 NW 23rd St., Oklahoma City

COST: Free to visit (entry is not allowed)

PRO TIP: Another Route 66 fixture, just down the street, Tower Theatre is a fully functioning live entertainment space dedicated to indie artists, inclusive programming, and themed dance nights.

Over the years, the Gold Dome has dodged the wrecking ball and been saved by impassioned preservationists. Whatever the future holds for Oklahoma City's most distinct building, be it another "bank of tomorrow" or another forward-thinking innovation, the dome still shines as an architectural star not just of Route 66 and Oklahoma, but of the world.

Located across the street, Milk Bottle Grocery is another quirky landmark (ca. 1930) that features a teeny 350-square-foot triangular brick building topped with a giant sheet-metal milk bottle, designed to advertise for the dairy industry.

OKLAHOMA'S NORDIC STONEHENGE

HEAVENER RUNESTONE PARK

WHAT: The site of a mysterious sandstone slab with Nordic carvings

WHERE: 18365 Runestone Rd., Heavener

COST: Free

PRO TIP: Heavener Runestone Park offers rentable sites for tents, RVs, and cabins, and reservations are recommended especially in the summer and fall.

Were Vikings the first Europeans to set foot in Oklahoma?

It's not too often a large slab of stone becomes a tourist attraction. In far eastern Oklahoma, though, a park unlike any other dwells atop Poteau Mountain.

Heavener Runestone Park, established in 1970, is oriented around a massive vertical sheet of sandstone, standing 10 feet wide and 12 feet tall. Aside from the sheer size, it's the carvings etched into it that are the real draw. Like hieroglyphics, the writing has been steeped in mystery ever since it was discovered by a Choctaw tribe in the 1830s. Initially nicknamed Indian Rock, for those who discovered it and the presumption that Native Americans were the ones who carved it, it wasn't until a century later that the story changed.

In 1928, a Heavener local named Gloria Farley noted that the carvings were akin to runic letters, leading her to surmise that Vikings actually traversed the area at one point—and that Vikings were the first Europeans to ever set foot in present-

Among the many other theories over the years as to the origins of the carvings, theorists have suggested they were left by anyone from the Irish to the Egyptians to the Knights Templar.

Photos courtesy of Lori Duckworth/Oklahoma Tourism

day Oklahoma. Over the years, more theories emerged, with some claiming a Swedish captain left them while guiding German colonizers through the Mississippi Valley in the 1700s.

The Smithsonian Institution shed some light when they categorized the markings, which spelled out "GNOMEDAL," as Scandinavian runes. According to the runic Scandinavian alphabet, that suggests the markings were meant to mean "sundial valley" or "monument valley." This was only to be refuted in 1986, when a professor at the University of Denmark suggested that the carving spelled "GLOMEDAL," indicating some kind of land claim.

Whatever the reality, the allure remains a wellspring of awe. The park today, overseen by the nonprofit group Friends of Heavener Runestone, contends that the markings were boundary markers left by Vikings between the years 600 and 800 AD. The stone is surrounded by a 55-acre park, with two miles of hiking trails, a waterfall, and a scenic overlook from atop the mountain. Heavener Runestone Park also holds periodic events like "May the Thor Be with You" races and an annual Viking Festival.

HAR-BER VILLAGE MUSEUM

WHAT: Pioneer-era history is on display at this six-acre lakeside village.

WHERE: 4404 W 20th St., Grove

COST: Fee varies for adults, free for children 5 and younger

PRO TIP: A newer addition is the Har-Ber Village Mining Company, which lets kids and families pan for minerals and gemstones.

A TASTE OF PIONEER PAST

How did a cabin community emerge in the middle of the woods?

In the mid-1800s, the eastern region of the state represented a bold new world for pioneers. It's all on display at seasonal Har-Ber Village, where nearly 100 exhibits and buildings make up a sprawling outdoor museum on the shores of Grand Lake o' the Cherokees.

Dating back to 1968, Har-Ber Village is the vision of Harvey and Bernice Jones, two Arkansas natives who created a portmanteau of their first names for the complex. Once they bought the land as a private lakeside retreat and built a church and cabin, curious passersby began to stop to see why old-timey buildings were starting to emerge in the woods. Far beyond a superficial homage, every facet of the village is of-the-era, starting with bricks that predate the Civil War, used to construct a church. From there, the couple added upwards

Courtesy of Har-Ber Village

Photos courtesy of Har-Ber Village

of 100 log cabins, linking them all via tree-lined walking paths with names like Memory Lane and Antique Alley. The cabins function as a makeshift town, representing everything that would have existed during the early pioneer days, including a doctor's office, courthouse, jail, mercantile, schoolhouse, and stagecoach inn. In between, museum displays are outfitted with everything from Civil War attire to vintage bathtubs and fine crystal goblets.

As more tourists visited, the village grew, with the Joneses adding to it from their personal collection back home in Arkansas. Nowadays, the village includes a nearly two-mile nature trail and a café, along with interactive exhibits, like water pumps and a cow-milking station, plus historical reenactments involving everything from puppets to covered wagons. Pioneer Days takes place annually in September, featuring living-history demonstrations and activities aplenty, and Civil War Era Historical Days is held in April.

Har-Ber Village is open seasonally, from March until November. There's also a country store, stocked with pioneer-era ephemera, for souvenirs and snacks.

In the area, be sure to check out Lendonwood Gardens, a three-acre botanical garden designed by retired dentist Dr. Leonard Miller and containing both American and Japanese gardening displays.

THE LAND-LOCKED LIGHTHOUSE

Why is there a working lighthouse on a reservoir in the middle of Oklahoma?

Lighthouses are seaside towers designed to provide guidance for ships and sailors. Lined up and down the coasts, with a historic concentration of them in New England, these nautical skyscrapers aren't mainstays in the middle of the country, because—literally—there's no need. How then did a replica of one of America's oldest lighthouses wind up on the shores of Oklahoma City's mightiest man-made reservoir?

Located on the east side of Lake Hefner, home to recreation activities like kayaking, cycling, and wind-surfing, the 36-foot-tall Lake Hefner Lighthouse beckons like an odd beacon from the end of a 75-yard jetty. Built in 1999, it's modeled after the Brant Point Light in Nantucket, which, built in 1746, is the second oldest lighthouse in the country. That light station has undergone several reincarnations, due mostly to weather damage, but its current tower—built in 1901—serves as direct source material for Lake Hefner. Ten feet taller than its Nantucket inspiration, the Oklahoma City attraction was initially nothing more than a photo opportunity.

That is, until an actual light was added to the lighthouse. Regardless of geography or oceanic proximity, the only thing distinguishing a "real" lighthouse from a fake one is

---

One other lighthouse in Oklahoma, the Centennial Lighthouse, rises 42 feet over a pond in Elk City, designed to celebrate the centennial of the state's admission into the Union in 1907.

a functioning red light. Now, the lighthouse shines at night, and it's even registered as a private aide to navigation with the Coast Guard. Unlike most lighthouses, which are built by the government, Lake Hefner's was a private structure that needed to be registered.

Unlike its historic kin on the coasts, the Lake Hefner Lighthouse does not have any adjoining gift shop or museum, nor can visitors enter. However, it functions much the same way it was originally intended: as a photo opportunity. At the end of a stone-lined jetty, with bench seating and panoramic views of the lake, it's one of the most photogenic spots in Oklahoma City. Nearby restaurants, including Redrock Canyon Grill and Mama Roja, provide beautiful views from their patios.

LAKE HEFNER LIGHTHOUSE

WHAT: An active lighthouse provides navigation and Nantucket vibes on a manmade reservoir.

WHERE: Lake Hefner Pkwy., Oklahoma City

COST: Free

PRO TIP: The best views are around sunset, from the outdoor patio and bar area at Redrock Canyon Grill.

Courtesy of Lori Duckworth/Oklahoma Tourism

LITTLE SAHARA STATE PARK

WHAT: Wind-swept dunes create the most "active" state park in Oklahoma.

WHERE: 8951 US Hwy. 281, Waynoka

COST: Fee for drivers and passengers

PRO TIP: Nearby companies, like Stewart Sandsports, offer rentals for ATVs.

DESERT DUNES IN THE PLAINS

Did camels help create Little Sahara?

At the confluence of the Midwest, the South, and the Southwest, Oklahoma's geography is hard to define, but dunes of quartz sand probably don't come to mind. Little Sahara State Park contains only 1,600 acres near the northwestern town of Waynoka, but there's something about its transportive landscape that feels out of place for the Great Plains. And it all started with a couple of camels.

Before the dunes were a state park, the local chamber of commerce—spearheaded by entrepreneurial local Grace Ward Smith—bought two camels from the Al G. Kelly Miller Brothers Circus, which was wintering in the Oklahoma town of Hugo in 1958, and released them into the dunes. The goal

Courtesy of Lori Duckworth/Oklahoma Tourism

Courtesy of Lori Duckworth/Oklahoma Tourism

was to drum up wildlife tourism, feature the camels in an "Oasis Pasture," and shed light on the sandy region.

A year later, the state legislature bought land to create a park to preserve acres of land marked by wind-blown sand—a frequent phenomenon alongside Oklahoma riverbanks in this part of the wind-swept state. Described as "active" dunes, which means the gusty sand cannot support vegetation, the sand ranges between 25 feet thick to 75 feet.

Most dunes come from ancient terrace deposits from when the Cimarron River once flowed through during Pleistocene times. This, coupled with ongoing sand blown from the present-day riverbanks, results in a dune system that is ever-changing. As sand flows northward, pouring down the opposing slopes, the entire "desert" inches along with it. The steady northeastern migration has resulted in the relocation of US Highway 281 three times over the past 70 years due to dune movement.

Little Sahara is mostly known as an ATV destination, but it also offers campsites and picnic tables. Because of all the dune buggy activity, hiking in the dunes is not permitted. The camels may be long gone, but Oklahoma's most otherworldly state park needs to be seen to be believed.

The camels, Susie and Nellie, remained in Little Sahara for years. They starred in Waynoka's Christmas pageant in the dunes in 1960, attracting a crowd of 4,000.

A GRAVE FIT FOR A HORSE

Is the real Mister Ed buried in Tahlequah?

Among the most famed equines to ever trot, Mister Ed was a palomino who rose to fame over six seasons—and 143 episodes—of his namesake TV series in the '60s. The horse, played by Bamboo Harvester and voiced by Allan "Rocky" Lane, talked exclusively to his owner, Wilbur Post, earning the character a place in comedic Hollywood lore. The only thing more curious than a chatty horse, though, is a chatty horse that may or may not be buried on private property in eastern Oklahoma.

Here, a five-foot granite grave displays an image of Mister Ed poking his head through a barn door. But how did the Hollywood horse, who lived and worked in California, wind up in rural Oklahoma? And is the horse buried here even really Mister Ed?

Most folks believe that the horse buried in Tahlequah is indeed Mister Ed. Born in 1949, he "retired" to the quiet Oklahoma farm after the show ended in 1966. It's common lore that Mister Ed got sick in 1968 and was euthanized, but

MISTER ED'S GRAVE

WHAT: The final resting place for Hollywood's most famous equine

WHERE: 13600 E 710 Rd., Tahlequah

COST: Free

PRO TIP: The grave is on private property, so be sure to get permission from the friendly owners by stopping by their home first.

Home to some 249,000 horses, Oklahoma is the fifth most horse-populated state in the nation, and the sixth in terms of human-to-horse ratio, with about one horse for every 10.8 people.

Courtesy of Tahlequah Area Chamber of Commerce

according to Alan Young, the actor who played Mister Ed's co-star, the horse died in California, where his ashes were given to trainer Lester Hilton. The horse buried in Tahlequah, he says, is a lookalike named Pumpkin, who subbed in for Mister Ed for publicity photos. The two horses appeared nearly identical, save for a gold spot on Pumpkin's mane. Contrary reports, though, theorize that Hilton took his horse with him to visit relatives in Oklahoma, leaving him there for a quieter life in retirement.

The grave was a simple wooden cross with a horseshoe, until the headstone was added in 1990, engraved with Mister Ed's likeness. Today, it acknowledges the mystery, while honoring the legacy: "According to media reports, Mr. Ed moved to Oklahoma in the late 1960s, after a successful Hollywood career. Mr. Ed continued to entertain and bring joy to many Oklahomans, finally retiring in this very field. May his memory live long."

NO MAN'S LAND

Is the Oklahoma panhandle as mysterious as they say?

Courtesy of Lori Duckworth/Oklahoma Tourism

For centuries, Oklahoma's 34-mile-wide panhandle was shrouded in mystery. Since Paleoindians first inhabited the region some 10,000 years ago, it's been populated by nomadic hunters and Indigenous tribes, like Apaches and Comanches. Texas originally took control of the present-day panhandle in 1836, only for it to be ceded as "public land" 14 years later. In 1854, the US government classified the panhandle vaguely as a "public land strip," which remained loosely defined until Cherokees claimed portions of the land, and the US Postal Service established offices postmarked with the Neutral Strip of Indian Territory. However, by 1885, the federal government had declared that the neutral strip was public land, invalidating squatters' homes. In 1886, the term "no man's land" was applied for the first time, and the region remains the last tract of "no man's land" left in the US.

Although the panhandle was incorporated with the rest of Oklahoma when it joined the Union in 1907, the land remains as mysterious and vague as ever—a notion exemplified by not only the lack of population and attractions but also the emergence of the No Man's Land Museum in 1934.

An extension of the Oklahoma Panhandle State University in Goodwell (population: 924) and operated in part by the Oklahoma Historical Society, the scrappy museum hearkens mostly to Oklahoma's Wild West pioneer era, along with oddities and kitsch, like a two-headed cow, dinosaur footprints, and a horse-drawn hearse, and lots of lore from the Dust Bowl. You'll also find Native American art and artifacts, from arrowheads to peace pipes to quills made from porcupines.

Photos courtesy of Lori Duckworth/ Oklahoma Tourism

It's all the handiwork of founders who were pre-statehood settlers—who participated in the Great Land Rush, endured the Dust Bowl, and settled in the wildest, weirdest part of the new state.

NO MAN'S LAND MUSEUM

WHAT: A ramshackle museum celebrating the mysterious pioneer-era history of the Oklahoma panhandle

WHERE: 214 East Ave., Goodwell

COST: Free

PRO TIP: There's a No Man's Land Historical Marker on the side of US Highway 64, which lists the historical towns and sites in the panhandle.

During the murky years when the panhandle didn't belong to any state, residents living there commonly used the phrase, "No Man's Land, but God's Land."

A TALL DRINK OF SODA

Would you dare to drink ranch dressing soda?

From blue whales to round barns, the Oklahoma portion of Route 66 has no shortage of roadside kitsch. Chief among the attractions, though, is an unmissable icon that looms large over the northeast suburbs of Oklahoma City: the world's largest soda bottle, which rises an apt 66 feet and illuminates at night, casting a glow over the quirky soda wonderland that is Pops 66.

While relatively young by Route 66 standards, established in 2007, Pops 66 quickly cemented itself as a road trip staple, as a one-stop-shop for gas and food, but especially for the neon-lit soda bottle that looms over the sprawling property. The whole aesthetic, designed by architect Rand Elliott, looks like a contemporary, Jetsons-style approach to Route 66 Americana, with the main building composed of sleek metal and glass, and hundreds of bottles of soda lining the window shelves, arranged by color. Altogether, there's about 700 different sodas here, doubling as wall art and drinks. Of the available sodas in the

Courtesy of Lori Duckworth/Oklahoma Tourism

Courtesy of Lori Duckworth/Oklahoma Tourism

coolers, all arranged by color, they run the gamut from vintage classics, like old-school sarsaparilla and grape soda, to oddities like sweet corn, PB&J, maple bacon, and even savory options like ranch dressing. There are over 80 different varieties of root beer alone, and guests will also find rare sodas from other countries. Altogether, Pops sources sodas from 13 countries, with the farthest distance being Bundaberg sodas from Australia. Despite its soda focus, the attraction isn't named after pop, but rather for the nickname that Pops's founder Aubrey McClendon had for his father.

To match, the full-service, diner-style restaurant serves soda-friendly Americana, like burgers and hot dogs, along with soda-centric sweets, like root beer bread pudding and ice cream floats. Out front, though, is where the most famous soda bottle can be found. Made with four tons of metal rings lined with LED lights, it's a striking feat of ingenuity and modern Route 66 innovation—which gets all the more photogenic after sunset.

Despite being pretty new, the gas station was designed specifically to replicate vintage service stations along the Mother Road, implementing a framed overhang that covers the '60s-style pump stations.

POPS 66

WHAT: The world's tallest soda bottle can be found in front of this soda-centric Route 66 fixture.

WHERE: 660 W Highway 66, Arcadia

COST: Free to visit (entree prices vary)

PRO TIP: Visit after sunset to see the 66-foot-tall soda bottle lit up with LED lights. The restaurant is open until 9 p.m., making it a great spot for a casual dinner or dessert.

FRANK LLOYD WRIGHT'S TALLEST MASTERPIECE

What inspired one of America's most famed architects to design his most ambitious project in Oklahoma?

PRICE TOWER

WHAT: The only skyscraper designed by Frank Lloyd Wright

WHERE: 510 Dewey Ave., Bartlesville

COST: Fee for guided tours

PRO TIP: Travelers can check out an homage to the Price Tower in Oklahoma City, where the 20-story Classen apartment tower replicates Wright's sky-scraping masterpiece.

Rising 19 stories over the rolling plains of northeastern Oklahoma, Frank Lloyd Wright's sole skyscraper was designed for Harold C. Price, who sought a headquarters site for his pipeline construction company. The general form for Price Tower was already in the hopper, as Wright had designed something similar for New York City in 1929, before the Great Depression squandered his plans for St. Mark's Tower. When Price commissioned Wright, the project presented Wright with the boldest opportunity of his illustrious career: a 19-story, 221-foot-tall skyscraper that could leave an indelible mark on Oklahoma.

The tower was constructed between 1953 and 1956, becoming the tallest building in

Courtesy of Lori Duckworth/Oklahoma Tourism

Bruce Goff, a native Oklahoman and a Frank Lloyd Wright protege, lived and worked in the Price Tower for nine years.

the oil-boom town. Wright had long championed the idea of nature as architectural inspiration, using elements that bring the outside in, and this was a sentiment enforced by the four elevator shafts as "roots," the cantilevered concrete floors as branches, and copper panels lining the tower as leaves. Similar to a tree, the tower grows narrower toward the top.

Functioning as a standalone neighborhood, the tower featured a car park, dress shop, salon, and the offices for the Public Service Company of Oklahoma. The top seven floors were reserved for the Price Company, with the penthouse functioning as Price's office suite. Wright also designed the decor, incorporating mid-century murals, triangular windows, upholstery, and chairs.

Price Tower opened in 1956 and was listed by the American Institute of Architects as one of Wright's most important creations. Although the Price company vacated the building in 1981, architecture tours commenced in 1987, followed by the debut of the Bartlesville Museum and Sculpture Garden in 1990 and the Inn at Price Tower in 2003. The tower still functions as a hotel today, along with Copper Restaurant + Bar and two floors' worth of gallery and exhibition space. The upper floors are available only for guided tours.

Courtesy of Lori Duckworth/Oklahoma Tourism

RIVERSPORT OKC

WHAT: A riverside adventure course with white water rapids, ziplines, surfing, and much more

WHERE: 800 Riversport Dr., Oklahoma City

COST: Prices vary for day passes

PRO TIP: Riversport OKC also provides equipment rentals and outings on Lake Hefner and Lake Overholser.

OLYMPIC RAPIDS IN THE PLAINS

How did the Olympics help develop one of the most unique water parks in the nation?

Ever since Oklahoma's Jim Thorpe became the first Native American to win an Olympic medal in 1912, the state has hovered on the Olympic radar—but always the bridesmaid, never the bride. A century later, the Oklahoma City Boathouse District has served as an Official US Olympic and Paralympic Training Site since 2009, making the Oklahoma River the only river in the country to earn such a role, while the Devon Boathouse operates as a National High Performance Center for US Rowing.

It all marks a culmination for a once-blighted stretch of water that stood more like stagnant drainage than river. That is, until the first phase of Oklahoma City's Metropolitan Area Projects Plan (MAPS) dammed portions of the Oklahoma River to create an urban training facility for athletes with Olympic aspirations. Now, the Oklahoma River provides training ground for rowers, kayaks, and canoes, along with contemporary infrastructure—including an indoor rowing tank

---

Each white water rapid pump at Riversport OKC circulates 82,000 gallons per minute, for a total of 492,000 gallons every 60 seconds—making it the highest volume white water channel on Earth.

Courtesy of Visit OKC

and exercise equipment designed for paddling—fully stocked with equipment and facilities.

The Devon Boathouse particularly, a $10 million, 33,000-square-foot facility, features everything from a rowing tank and a high-altitude training room to an indoor propulsion swimming pool and sports medicine resources. Outside, the river is now flowing at its fullest potential, including an eight-lane, 2,000-meter race course for rowers. The region's infamous wind provides a challenge, mild winters allow for year-round training, and stadium lights keep things operational for night races.

Beyond the Olympic training facilities, the Boathouse District developed a veritable riverside amusement park in Riversport OKC. The attraction is home to the world's tallest adventure course, including a Sky Slide and 700-foot zipline. Closer to Earth, there's a kayak center, surf simulator, skiing simulator, and $45 million white water rafting course, allowing adrenaline-junkies to experience Class IV rapids with skyline views.

Courtesy of Visit OKC

OKLAHOMA'S STAR ASTRONAUT

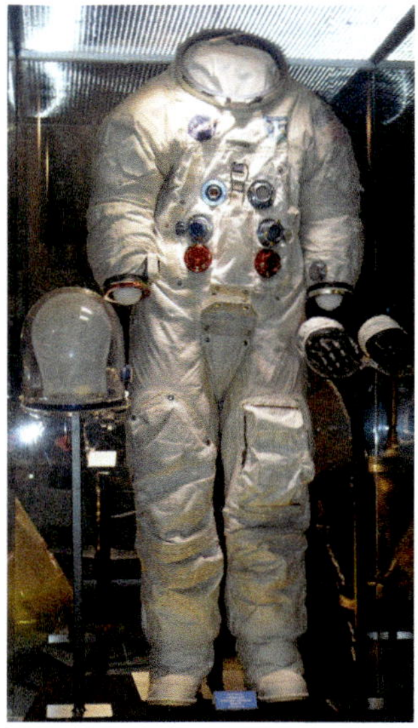

Courtesy of Stafford Air and Space Museum

How did Thomas Stafford go from climbing windmills to orbiting the moon and running Area 51?

Thomas Stafford is an Oklahoma-born astronaut whose legacy is the stuff of sci-fi lore. Born and raised in Weatherford, he joined the US Naval Academy, going on to become a three-star general in the US Air Force, and the first general to go into space. Stafford was one of only 24 astronauts to ever go to the moon, and while he never walked on it, he flew two Gemini rendezvous missions and commanded the Apollo 10 mission—the first successful launch of a lunar module into orbit. Before Armstrong and Aldrin landed on the moon, he orbited within nine miles of its surface in 1969, officially achieving President John F. Kennedy's goal to beat the Soviet Union in the "Space Race" to the moon. Upon his descent, he set the record for fastest human speed, clocking in at a staggering 24,791 mph.

Back on Earth, Stafford became the chief of the Astronaut Office for NASA, chaired the crew that developed Hubble's COSTAR (Corrective Optics Space Telescope Axial Replacement), and even worked at Area 51. There, he served as the commanding general of the top-secret facility, working on classified experimental technology referred to as Stealth, and developing both the F-117 Stealth Fighter and B-2 Stealth Bomber. This earned Stafford the nickname as the Air Force's "Father of Stealth."

He also co-commanded the final Apollo mission, Apollo-Soyuz, in a joint mission with Soviet crew member Alexei Leonov

Courtesy of Stafford Air and Space Museum

to help end the Cold War. For these efforts, he was nominated for a Nobel Peace Prize.

Stafford's legacy is celebrated at the Stafford Air & Space Museum in Weatherford. What started as a six-foot display case in the Weatherford airport in the '70s has expanded into a 63,000-square-foot facility, with a Lockheed F-104 "Starfighter" outside, and exhibits paying homage to Stafford's legacy, including a Titan II rocket, Stafford's own pressure suits, and shuttles. It's the only museum in the world with engines from the US Saturn V and Soviet N-1 moon rockets from the famed "Space Race."

STAFFORD AIR & SPACE MUSEUM

WHAT: A Smithsonian-affiliated museum dedicated to one of the most legendary astronauts to ever circle the moon

WHERE: 3000 Logan Rd., Weatherford

COST: Fee for entry, free for active military and kids 5 and younger

PRO TIP: The Stafford Air & Space Museum regularly hosts space camps and events, like book signings with astronauts, so check the museum website and social media to see what's happening.

In 1965, Stafford played the first song in space. After rendezvousing with Gemini VII in December, he and crewmate Walter "Wally" Schirra played "Jingle Bells" with instruments they snuck onboard, joking to mission control that they had spotted Santa Claus. Those instruments are now on display at the National Air and Space Museum.

A CAVE FOR OUTLAWS

Is there hidden treasure in the wilderness of southeastern Oklahoma?

Before Oklahoma joined the Union, the mountainous southeastern part of the territory was the perfect all-natural hideaway. For its dense forests and murky caves, present-day Robbers Cave State Park became a go-to grotto for outlaws on the run. Some of the most infamous, like Jesse James and Belle Starr, were said to have hidden here, thanks to the park's namesake cave, which extends 40 feet into a mountain.

Initially, this region was used as an Osage hunting ground and later an area of exploration for French settlers. It reached peak infamy, however, when Jesse James arrived. Although the gangster was not from Oklahoma, he often retreated here

In addition to Robbers Cave, outlaws also retreated to other hideaways in Oklahoma, like a log cabin nestled at the base of nearby Sugar Loaf Mountain, where both Jesse James and Belle Starr were known to have gone.

Courtesy of Lori Duckworth/Oklahoma Tourism

due to the lack of regulation. Being acutely familiar with the cave, which allegedly contained a hidden rear escape exit, the terrain provided an advantage for criminals.

After James's death in 1882, the buried treasure mythos died with him. The development of Oklahoma meant that many of these once-remote hiding places were lost to time. James's brother, Frank, returned to Oklahoma several times in search of their stowed treasures, only to come up empty-handed.

Gold or not, Robbers Cave has become a treasure in Oklahoma. The land was donated to the Boy Scouts of America in 1929 and designated Camp Tom Hale, until the development and acquisition of nearby land—spurred by President Franklin D. Roosevelt's New Deal Program—led to the creation of Latimer State Park. The name was changed to Robbers Cave partly due to the region's infamous lore, and it became one of Oklahoma's original state parks in 1936. Nowadays, the park is far more developed than it once was, featuring cabins, yurts, playgrounds, trails (including the aptly dubbed Outlaws Nature Trail), and even a mini golf course.

ROBBERS CAVE STATE PARK

WHAT: A mountainous state park with infamous history as a hideaway for outlaws

WHERE: 2084 NW 146th Rd., Wilburton

COST: Free to visit

PRO TIP: An annual fall festival at Robbers Cave features hundreds of classic cars on display, plus live entertainment and food aplenty.

Photos courtesy of Lori Duckworth/ Oklahoma Tourism

A DISTILLERY WITH A PROHIBITIONIST PAST

Did a hatchet-wielding Kansan make Oklahoma a dry state?

Before Oklahoma joined the Union, much of the state was the Wild West—where criminals could run rampant, and transplants could help shape the shifting territory. Such was the case with Moses Weinberger, a Kansan who moved to Guthrie and opened the territory's first bar, Same Old Moses Saloon. Little did he know that he was inciting the wrath of a hatchet-wielding Prohibitionist, Carry Nation.

After Nation's husband died of alcoholism, she embarked on a crusade against alcohol. She began a women's temperance organization, the Workers for Christ, in Seiling, Oklahoma, decrying the sins of liquor, and developed a reputation for attacking saloons with hatchets. She advocated for Prohibition at various lectures, and through

THE WANDER INN

WHAT: The first legal distillery in Oklahoma is located in a historic building in downtown Guthrie.

WHERE: 118 E Oklahoma Ave., Guthrie

COST: Free to visit (cocktail prices vary)

PRO TIP: A great way to visit the Wander Inn is as part of a larger festival in Guthrie, like a bluegrass festival and wine festival, both held annually in the fall.

Leaning into the absurdity, Weinberger once invited Nation into his saloon to make a temperance speech, with the sole caveat that she not use a hatchet. Unfortunately, she didn't keep her promise, instead smashing a piece out of Weinberger's mahogany bar.

her own publication, *The Hatchet*, all while harassing local saloon owners like Weinberger. Cheekily, the latter hung a sign above his bar door that read, "All nations welcome, except Carry." When Oklahoma became a state in 1907, it did so as a dry one, and Same Old Moses shut its doors for good.

It set the tone for nearly a century of liquor laws that restricted bars, breweries, and until recently, distilleries. In Guthrie, WanderFolk Spirits is the first legal distillery in the state. Once it became legal to make alcohol in 2012, more than a century after statehood, the company began as Prairie Wolf Spirits, before evolving into WanderFolk.

Leaning into the lore, the company features Same Old Moses bourbon and a line of Garden Club spirits, named after the horticultural hobby groups formed by Guthrie's Prohibitionist women. Today, the WanderFolk Spirits distillery is located next door to the Wander Inn, a cocktail bar utilizing spirits made on the other side of the wall. And to this day, all nations are welcome at the Wander Inn, except Carry.

Photos courtesy of WanderFolk Spirits

THE SKINNIEST STRETCH OF ROUTE 66

Why is the "Sidewalk Highway" so narrow?

Route 66 extends more than 2,400 miles, but there's one stretch that stands out for its diminutive size. Ribbon Road is the thinnest part of the entire thoroughfare, with history that predates the route entirely.

In northeastern Oklahoma, a section of the road is about half the size of the rest of it. Ribbon Road, aka Sidewalk Highway, is so named for the fact that—at nine feet wide—it's approximately the width of a sidewalk.

Weaving through rural farmland near Miami, Ribbon Road was designed and paved years before Route 66. Mapped in 1921, a good five years before the rest of the route, the narrow section stretched for 15 miles between Miami and Afton. The reason for the width? The newly minted state didn't have the funds for full highway-sized roads.

Made with concrete and asphalt, the road was sufficient for the lack of automobiles at the time. Infrequent traffic meant that, even at half the size of a standard two-lane road, cars would rarely cross paths, and if they did, it was easy enough to pull over and let someone pass. In 1926, upon completion of Route 66, Ribbon Road was absorbed into the rest of the highway, where it remained a part of the itinerary until it was realigned in 1937.

RIBBON ROAD LANDMARK

WHAT: The thinnest part of historic Route 66 is the width of an average sidewalk

WHERE: E 140 Rd., Miami

COST: Free

PRO TIP: Find sections of Ribbon Road remnants on East 140 Road south of Miami, and look for the highway marker at the corner of Highway 59. The road is pretty gnarly nowadays, so be sure to drive carefully.

Courtesy of Rhys Martin

Although Ribbon Road is no longer technically part of Route 66, and much of the Sidewalk Highway has been undone by overuse, there are still two sections that travelers can drive, one covering about three miles south of Miami and the other in Narcissa. Between Miami and Afton, a Ribbon Road Highway Landmark greets passersby on the side of the small highway.

Due to its size, and the fact that it's mostly trafficked by farm equipment, Ribbon Road has faced considerable wear and tear over the years, to the point where preservationists have convened to help save it. It is listed on the National Register of Historic Places, and Ottawa County officials are working on plans to rehabilitate the Sidewalk Highway.

Ribbon Road exited Route 66 in 1937, when Governor E. W. Marland cut the ribbon (ironically) on the Neosho River Bridge, linking a new—and widened—stretch of highway, officially making every mile of the Mother Road a two-lane paved route.

JURASSIC MUSEUM

What kinds of dinosaurs once roamed Oklahoma?

Oklahoma wasn't always the wind-swept plains that it is today, but rather a veritable Jurassic Park of some of the largest beasts on the fossil record. All of which are preserved at the Sam Noble Museum.

Founded in 1899 as the Department of Geology and Natural History by the Territorial Legislature, on the University of the Territory of Oklahoma campus, its function is to preserve the natural resources and human cultural heritage from the earliest days of life in present-day Oklahoma. This includes dinosaurs so epic they make bison look like bunnies. Fossils excavated in the state are some of the largest ever discovered—including wooly mammoths, a fearsome apatosaurus, and a super-sized T-rex known as Saurophaganax maximus, all of which once roamed these lands. The museum's pentaceratops, an herbivorous

---

The panhandle was where some of the largest fossil specimens were found, and the best place to see preserved dinosaur tracks in the wild is near Black Mesa State Park.

Courtesy Lori Duckworth/Oklahoma Tourism

dinosaur similar to a triceratops, holds the record for the largest dinosaur skull ever discovered.

Collections grew under Dr. Albert Heald Van Vleet, who accumulated items from the 1904 St. Louis World's Fair and Oklahoma's Spiro Mounds. As collections grew and fossils got bigger, more space was needed. When a $10 million donation came from the Samuel R. Noble Foundation, named after an Oklahoma oilman and philanthropist, the museum's name was changed to its current moniker. Groundbreaking for the new 198,000-square-foot facility took place in 1996, and it opened in 2000.

The museum contains more than 10 million items—spanning 500 million years of Oklahoma history—within 50,000 square feet of exhibit space. A bulk of the museum is dedicated to dinosaurs, and there's also a painted 10,000-year-old bison skull, making it the oldest painted object on the continent. The Hall of the People of Oklahoma is an homage to human history in the state, with Indigenous roots extending back 30,000 years. Visitors will find handprints from 26 of the state's 39 tribes and immersive displays like pole houses and cedar canoes.

SAM NOBLE MUSEUM

WHAT: The original Department of Geology and Natural History contains billions of years of prehistoric lore.

WHERE: 2401 Chautauqua Ave., Norman

COST: Fees vary for entry

PRO TIP: Also at the University of Oklahoma is the Fred Jones Jr. Museum of Art, containing 20,000 items in a permanent collection of French Impressionism, Native American art, Asian graphics, and more.

Courtesy of Lori Duckworth/ Oklahoma Tourism

LAND OF 10,000 (MANMADE) LAKES

LAKES

WHAT: Oklahoma has more manmade lakes than any other state.

WHERE: Multiple locations. Eufaula Lake: Eufaula, 74432,Tenkiller Ferry Lake: 446977 E 980 Rd.

COST: Prices vary

PRO TIP: Oklahoma Lake is a privately owned lake that costs $10 per person and contains campsites, picnic tables, various beaches, and—in the summer months—a giant slide.

Does Oklahoma have more shoreline than any other state?

Home to 55,000 miles of shoreline, more than the Atlantic and Gulf Coasts combined, Oklahoma is the most unexpected watery wonderland. Water covers 1,224 square miles—or more than 1 million acres—in the land-locked state. Much of that number is manufactured, though, as Oklahoma contains more manmade lakes than any other state.

With more than 200 manmade lakes, nearly the entirety of Oklahoma's shoreline is artificial. But nonetheless, the state has emerged as a playground for water sports, from wind-surfing and swimming to kayaking, paddle-boarding, and scuba diving.

The Oklahoma Water Resources Board reports that the state has about 3,000 lakes and ponds, amounting to more

---

When President Lyndon B. Johnson dedicated the Eufaula Dam in 1964, it created the largest-capacity lake in Oklahoma, reaching a depth of 87 feet and capable of generating 90,000 kilowatts of hydroelectric power.

Courtesy of Visit OKC

than 55,000 miles of shoreline. For comparison, Alaska boasts 33,904 miles of shoreline. Most were created by the US Army Corps of Engineers, the Grand River Dam Authority, and the US Bureau of Reclamation for flood control, drinking water, hydroelectric power, and recreation.

Oklahoma's largest lakes—all man-made—are Lake Eufaula, Lake Tenkiller, and Grand Lake. The former contains more than 600 miles of shoreline and covers 102,200 acres of surface area (the most in the state). With crystalline waters, Lake Tenkiller is popular for fishing and scuba diving, while parasailing is a pastime at Grand Lake. Straddling the Texas border, Lake Texoma has the largest volume of water in Oklahoma.

Manmade lakes come in all shapes and sizes. Lake Hefner covers four square miles in Oklahoma City and serves as both a reservoir and recreation destination. The same is true of Lake Overholser in Oklahoma City, Arcadia Lake in Edmond, and Lake Stanley Draper in Norman. With 86 miles of shoreline, Lake Thunderbird is another mighty body of water, with two marinas and two swimming beaches.

The only natural bodies of water in Oklahoma are small oxbow and playa lakes, which are usually found in flood plains of major rivers. The largest natural lake, an offshoot of the Red River, measures about 272 acres in McCurtain County.

Courtesy of Visit OKC

THE OZARK TRAIL

WHAT: A scenic thoroughfare that predates Route 66

WHERE: Throughout Oklahoma

COST: Free

PRO TIP: Broadway Avenue is a brick-lined road in Davenport, from the original Ozark Trail, that stands as another preserved remnant on the National Register of Historic Places.

TRACING THE OZARK TRAIL

Did you know the Mother Road wasn't the only iconic highway in Oklahoma?

Everyone knows about Route 66, but far fewer know about another scenic roadway, which came before and set the precedent for the Mother Road to follow years later.

The Ozark Trail took shape in 1913, designed to connect St. Louis with southwestern cities like Santa Fe and El Paso, meandering through Oklahoma along its westward route. Riding the wave of automobile development, the trail formally existed from 1915 until 1926, right when Route 66 was completed (Oklahomans owned about 60,000 cars by the time the trail began), and some of the Ozark Trail's roads were absorbed into the larger thoroughfare.

Spurred by the Good Roads Association and Oklahoma's transportation department, with the goal of improving roadways and car travel in and around the state, the Ozark Trail was one of the first "national highways" advanced by the US Bureau of Public Roads. The route was named by Arkansan William Harvey, who worked with Oklahoman Cyrus Avery to map out the Oklahoma portion of the route, which included a well-trafficked section between Sapulpa and Oklahoma City. Deliberately designed to be slow and scenic, roads regularly came to 90-degree turns, and much of the itinerary was lined with telephone poles painted green and white, and eventually, white obelisks with green letters.

Courtesy of Oklahoma Tourism

Upon the completion of Route 66 in 1926, the US Office of Public Roads absorbed much of the Ozark Trail into the new route. Although most of the trail has faded to time, a roadside obelisk remains at the intersection of County Roads E0890 and N3540 near Stroud, and another near Langston, at the intersection of Indian Meridian Road and Washington Avenue. The Stroud section is now listed on the National Register of Historic Places.

Rock Creek Bridge, established in 1921, was part of both the Ozark Trail and Route 66 until 1952, and it still stands in Sapulpa as a quintessential example of steel-truss architecture.

OKLAHOMA'S MOST HAUNTED HOTEL

Courtesy of Oklahoma Historical Society

Who is the chambermaid who haunts the Skirvin?

When the Skirvin Hotel opened in Oklahoma City in 1911, the Art Deco property—realized by entrepreneur William Balser Skirvin, who came to Oklahoma for the Land Rush of 1889—towered at a then-staggering 14 stories. Designed by architect Solomon Andrew Layton, plans called for a six-story hotel in the shape of a "U," but the architect convinced Skirvin to go bigger. Upon completion, the 225-room hotel offered not only the largest hotel in town but also the finest hotel in the Southwest, designed with English Gothic interiors.

The hotel attracted bigwigs, politicians, and cultured travelers. Bank robbers were even said to hang out here, and gun-toting shootouts were not a rare occurrence. Demand was so high that Skirvin added a 12-story wing, bringing the room total to 525 by 1930. Although Skirvin's children sold the property after his death in 1945, it continued to attract the same debutantes and dignitaries—everyone from Elvis Presley to President Eisenhower have visited. Skirvin's daughter, Perle Mesta, even became the ambassador to Luxembourg under President Truman, another guest at the hotel. But it's another

---

James Beard Award-winning chef Andrew Black opened an homage to the hotel's past at Perle Mesta, an on-site restaurant named for the hotelier's daughter.

figure who commands the most attention—from beyond the grave.

Effie is a chambermaid who worked at the Skirvin during Prohibition. While the hotelier lived on-site in a five-room suite, the two were said to have had an affair, resulting in a child. Rather than celebrate, she was locked away on the 10th floor until she could give birth in secret. Once the baby was born, she jumped to her death. To this day, guests report eerie sounds and sights, like doors slamming and babies crying. Some NBA teams, in town to play the Oklahoma City Thunder, have been so disturbed that they either opt to share rooms or insist on staying at another hotel.

The historic property closed temporarily in 1988, and reopened in 2007 after $50 million in renovations. But one thing that hasn't changed is that some ghosts never really go away.

THE SKIRVIN HOTEL

WHAT: The finest historic hotel in the Southwest may be haunted by a Prohibition-era chambermaid.

WHERE: One Park Ave., Oklahoma City

COST: Rates vary.

PRO TIP: Stop by the hotel's Red Piano Lounge for live music and a Wedding Cake Martini (or two).

Photos courtesy of Oklahoma Historical Society

SOLITARY SOD HOUSE

How—and why—did early pioneers build homes from grass?

Oklahoma Territory may have been settled swiftly during the various land rushes, but development was a slower burn. Before timber became readily available, settlers improvised with what was available, and in the case of the plains, that meant sod.

Prairie sod is a thick bed of roots made from grasses that evolved to become drought-resistant and hardy enough to serve as both foundation and insulation. Known as "soddies," sod houses were shelters, during the pre-timber days, for families, who constructed abodes that rose up to 14 feet tall and 16 feet wide.

Settlers used plows to cut sod into segments, roughly one foot wide and four inches thick, before using a spade to cut them into blocks. These were hauled to construction sites and stacked to build walls up to three feet thick. What limited wood pioneers were able to find were used as support poles, rafters, and doorframes. Meanwhile, interior walls were layered with plaster, windows were covered with oiled paper, and furnishings were sparse.

SOD HOUSE MUSEUM

WHAT: The only remaining sod house in Oklahoma is preserved in this humidity-controlled museum.

WHERE: 4628 OK-8, Aline

COST: Fee for entry

PRO TIP: The Sod House Museum has one staff member, so call ahead at 580-463-2441 to ensure you can visit.

One of the best ways to experience the museum is by participating in a quilting workshop, which the Sod House offers periodically throughout the year.

Photos courtesy of Lori Duckworth/Oklahoma Tourism

There were an estimated one million sod houses throughout the great plains. With the expansion of railroads, though, settlers became able to acquire timber, which signaled the beginning of the end for soddies. Today, one sod house remains in Oklahoma, and it's preserved in a temperature-controlled museum in Aline.

The Sod House Museum is a two-room house built in 1894 by Marshal McCully, who came to Oklahoma Territory when the Cherokee Outlet opened for settlement in 1893. Using sod made from buffalo grass, McCully and his family lived there until 1909, when—using newly available timber—they built a sturdier home nearby. Their original abode was used for storage until 1963 but has since been repurposed as a museum. The Oklahoma Historical Society acquired the property in 1963, building a cover structure in 1967 to protect it from the elements and opening it as a museum that same year.

ROOTS RUN DEEP AT THIS TALL PRAIRIE

How did Oklahoma protect the largest remaining tract of grassland in the world?

After the last Ice Age, when glaciers receded and left behind rich topsoil, tallgrass prairie flourished. Reaching up to six feet in height, tallgrass covered 170 million acres of North America—roughly one-third of the continent, from present-day Canada down to Texas. Today, though, only 4 percent remains, and the largest protected remnants are preserved in Oklahoma.

Eastern Oklahoma and Kansas contain a majority of the remaining tallgrass prairie, mostly due to the rocky terrain of the Flint Hills region where they grow, making them unusable for farmers or developers. These hearty plants, with roots that extend more than five feet underground, serve as food for native grazers, as shelter for nesting birds and migrating butterflies, and as a powerful

JOSEPH H. WILLIAMS TALLGRASS PRAIRIE PRESERVE

WHAT: This preserve in the Flint Hills protects the largest area of tallgrass prairie left on Earth.

WHERE: 15316 Co. Rd. 4201, Pawhuska

COST: Free

PRO TIP: Although bison are practically a guaranteed sight year-round, they are most active—and most visible—during mating season, from June to September.

Courtesy of Carmon Briggs

Courtesy of The Nature Conservancy

combatant against climate change. Compared to trees, tallgrass absorbs and retains more carbon in its root system, even after prescribed fires burn the portions of the plant on the surface. They may not boast the same obvious beauty of mountains or canyons, but tallgrass prairies are one of the most biodiverse ecosystems on Earth, second only to the Amazon rainforest.

They're also a sustainable resource for bison. At Oklahoma's Joseph H. Williams Tallgrass Prairie Preserve, which, at 40,000 acres, is the single largest protected portion of tallgrass prairie left on Earth, the marquee attraction is a herd of about 2,000 free-roaming bison. To conserve the delicate prairie, the herd is managed through annual roundups, wherein North America's largest land mammals are tagged, vaccinated, and tallied, with excessive numbers sold mostly to meat producers to ensure population health.

The preserve, overseen by the Nature Conservancy, is only partially accessible to visitors. That means the visitor center is open only occasionally; vehicles are not permitted on the preserve; dogs are not allowed on hiking trails; and camping, hunting, and fishing are prohibited. To experience tallgrass at its tallest, visit in the fall, when the amber plants can reach more than six feet tall.

Osage historian John Joseph Mathews offers monthly guided tours of a historic cabin on the preserve, where he used to live.

A BARN BUILT FOR DANCING

How did this Route 66 landmark get such a distinct shape?

William Harrison "Big Bill" Odor arrived in Oklahoma in 1892, claiming land in present-day Arcadia. By 1898, he had used oxen to plow and clear his land, with plans to construct a distinct kind of barn. Using local burr oak, Odor soaked strips of timber in water to make them malleable enough to force into curves and hold in a rounded shape.

Designed by Odor, the rounded barn is 60 feet wide and 43 feet tall, finished the same year it began, in 1898. Initially, Odor used it to store grain, hay, and livestock, but its shape endeared it for other uses.

During construction, three of the builders convinced Odor to open the space for community gatherings. They were so insistent that they offered to pay to upgrade the floor to hardwood, to make it more suitable for barn dances. Not only was the space unique, but its shape also helped with acoustics. Odor agreed, on the condition that "good music" be played. Almost immediately upon its completion, the barn became a destination for dances and soirees, with Odor even comparing the acoustics to that of the Mormon Tabernacle in Salt Lake City.

While Odor never confirmed his vision for the round barn, his son, Ralph, suggested it may have been due to tornadoes. While no scientific evidence exists to support the claim, it was thought at the time that round buildings were tornado-proof, and that storms would pass around them, rather than through.

After Route 66 was aligned through Arcadia in 1928, the barn took on a new purpose—as a roadside pitstop. The Arcadia Round Barn has been a requisite attraction along the Mother Road, with visitors free to go inside and take photos or test out the acoustics. It experienced a period of decay in the middle of the century, until its designation on the National Register of Historic Places in 1977 brought a fresh wave of restoration.

Nowadays, the only round barn in Oklahoma remains a mystery, but visitors are free to visit the property, which has a gift shop and museum on the ground floor and a level on the second floor for events, accessible to the public when not in use. To this day, barn dances (and other events) are still a recurring, timeworn feature at one of Oklahoma's strangest structures.

ARCADIA ROUND BARN

WHAT: One of the only rounded barns in the country sits on Route 66 just outside Oklahoma City.

WHERE: 107 OK-66, Arcadia

COST: Free

PRO TIP: Round Barn Rendezvous are held from noon until 4 p.m. on the second Sunday of every month, featuring open-mic acoustic performances from any musician looking to participate.

Courtesy of Oklahoma Tourism

CUSTER'S SECOND-TO-LAST STAND

Courtesy of Lori Duckworth/Oklahoma Tourism

What brought America's most infamous colonel to Oklahoma Territory?

Before Lieutenant Colonel George A. Custer made his march into the Battle of the Little Bighorn, America's most notorious warrior left his bloody mark on Native lands in western Oklahoma. The Battle of the Little Bighorn may have been his last stand, but the Battle of the Washita was the penultimate event that paved the way to his demise.

The Great Plains Wars were a stain in American history that saw the forced removal of Native tribes. Among the battles in Oklahoma Territory was that at Washita, where the US Army clashed with Southern Cheyenne and Southern Arapaho in a surprise attack.

Leading up to the battle in 1868, Major General Philip H. Sheridan sought new strategies in combating tribes defiant to gold rushers and settlers. Sheridan planned an assault later in the year, when the weather was cold and the tribes were more vulnerable, with Custer as his muscle. Following a tribal trail through the snow, Custer settled on a ridge in the morning hours of November 28. His target was Cheyenne peace chief Black Kettle and his camp of 250.

Although Black Kettle was tipped off by Colonel William B. Hazen, efforts proved futile. At dawn, the encampment was under assault in a matter of minutes. Arapaho and Kiowa fighters helped assist the Cheyenne in battle, but they couldn't prevent the brutal blow. Black Kettle was killed, along with

Courtesy of Lori Duckworth/Oklahoma Tourism

dozens more. Additionally, Custer's troops destroyed much of the encampment, and they took many prisoners as they marched back to camp that evening.

The Battle of Washita was Custer's final major battle until his last stand at Little Bighorn in 1876.

To remember his infamy, Washita Battlefield National Historic Site was designated in 1996, encompassing more than 300 acres, and a 1.5-mile trail that takes visitors to the site of the battle.

WASHITA BATTLEFIELD NATIONAL HISTORIC SITE

WHAT: Native American history is preserved at this national park site acknowledging the Great Plains Wars.

WHERE: 18555 OK-47 Alt, Cheyenne

COST: Free

PRO TIP: Previously a standalone museum nearby, the Black Kettle Museum has been absorbed into the visitor center facilities at the national park site, highlighting more history of the Cheyenne tribe in their battle against Custer.

Also overseen by the National Park Service, the Trail of Tears National Historic Trail includes Oklahoma sites significant to the forced migration of the Cherokee people, including their Webbers Falls settlement and the Cherokee Female Seminary in Tahlequah.

SPIRO MOUNDS

WHAT: Oklahoma's only prehistoric Native American archaeological site open to the public

Where: 18154 1st St., Spiro

Cost: Free

Pro Tip: Due to limited staffing at the archaeological center, it's recommended that visitors call ahead, at 918-962-2062, to check operating hours.

THE KING TUT OF OKLAHOMA

What happened to the lost civilization of the Spiro people?

Around 850 AD, Caddo people built ceremonial earthen mounds, using baskets of dirt, to create temples and homes. Most were used for residential purposes, but the burial mound—the Craig Mound—is where historical riches lay. Unbeknownst to the Choctaw and Chickasaw people in the late 1800s, beneath their feet lay one of the mightiest archaeological collections in history. Discovered in 1933, when the Pocola Mining Company leased the land, workers unearthed so many Native American artifacts that the *Kansas City Star* dubbed it the "King Tut of the Arkansas Valley."

Although miners damaged a good portion of the mound in the dig, they accessed a stunningly preserved collection of artifacts, from Florida conch shells to copper from the Great Lakes. Once the state legislature realized the value, they halted operations with the mining company, to prevent further damage.

Archaeologists from the University of Oklahoma stepped in, to catalog the findings, which included more than 600 burials and

Under the direction of the Pocola Mining Company, Spiro Mound artifacts were sold to museums across the US, Europe, and Asia, where they can still be found. To this day, it's the worst incident of archaeological looting in the nation's history.

Courtesy of Lori Duckworth/Oklahoma Tourism

thousands of artifacts. The US Army Corps of Engineers attempted to protect the land by creating a national archaeological park, and in 1978, the Spiro Mounds Archaeological State Park became the first and only prehistoric Native American archaeological site open to the public.

The discovery marked a turning point for one of the most influential ancient Native American civilizations. Spiro was the epicenter of the mound-building nations known as the Mississippian Culture, which reached three million people and 60 tribes. Its location on the Arkansas River made it a hub on an east-west trade route, but by 1250, a period of drought triggered the collapse of many Mississippian cities, including—by 1450—Spiro. Mounds were abandoned in search of more fruitful plains.

The Spiro Mounds Archaeological Center contains an interpretive center, along with a trail system that takes visitors out into the wilderness where the Mississippian Culture once thrived.

THE FIRST AMERICAN MARTYR

Is Oklahoma home to a saint?

Born in 1935 in Okarche, Oklahoma, Stanley Rother moved away to pursue the priesthood. By the time he returned home, he did so as an ordained Catholic priest in Oklahoma City, but it wasn't long before he was once again called on a mission.

He took a post in Guatemala, where he formed a bond with the native Tz'utujil people, Mayan descendants who often suffered from poverty but who found companionship in Father Rother. The priest helped with farming techniques he had learned in Oklahoma, and he became the first outsider to learn the Tz'utujil language. The Tz'utujil came to call him "Padre A'Plas," designating him a community elder.

Father Rother returned to Oklahoma during Guatemala's civil war. Despite his work to help the Natives, militant combatants sought to stifle his efforts. Oklahoma was a safer refuge, but he implored the bishop that he be allowed to return to his flock.

Return he did, only to meet a gristly fate. Father Rother was killed in 1981, shortly after returning to Guatemala. When three assailants

In the main chapel, a massive mural depicts numerous other martyrs from history, including Saints Thomas Becket, John Fisher, Oscar Romero, John the Baptist, and Joan of Arc.

Photos courtesy of Blessed Stanley Rother Shrine

BLESSED STANLEY ROTHER SHRINE

WHAT: A temple to the first native-born American to be beatified and declared a martyr

WHERE: 700 SE 89th St., Oklahoma City

COST: Free

PRO TIP: Blessed Stanley Rother Shrine also features an outdoor replica of Tepeyac Hill, complete with a 12-foot bronze statue of Our Lady of Guadalupe, modeled after the original in Mexico where Mary appeared to Saint Juan Diego in 1531.

came to kidnap him in the night, he refused to be taken and refused to make any noise, at the risk of waking any nuns. His last words were, "Kill me here," and he died in his church, shot twice. In mourning, his flock buried his heart beneath the church, while the rest of his body was buried in Okarche.

In 2016, the Vatican named Father Rother a martyr, and the following year, he was beatified in Oklahoma City, marking the final step before sainthood. To this day, he remains the only US-born priest to be beatified and martyred. The Blessed Stanley Rother Shrine and Museum, designed with the same Spanish Colonial style as his church in Guatemala, was dedicated in his honor on the southside of Oklahoma City in 2023. Visitors are welcome, and there's an on-site museum honoring the life and legacy of one of America's most hallowed shepherds.

INSIDE SCOOP ON *THE OUTSIDERS* HOUSE

How did Tulsa help birth the Brat Pack era?

After Tulsa author S. E. Hinton published *The Outsiders* in 1967, Francis Ford Coppola came to town to give it the movie treatment. *The Outsiders* movie was filmed entirely in Tulsa and released in 1983, featuring a cast of up-and-comers as famed as the director.

When Coppola adapted Hinton's book, he eschewed Hollywood sound stages for the real deal. He went right to the source material to tell the story of 14-year-old Ponyboy Curtis, his role in a local gang known as the Greasers, and their rivalry with another gang known as the Socs. To tell the story, the director took over a house in an ordinary Tulsa neighborhood, and turned it—and the surrounding area—into one giant movie set.

The "Curtis Brothers House," where the present-day museum dedicated to the film now sits, is a bungalow-style abode. It's where some of the brightest stars of the early '80s convened, including Rob Lowe, Emilio Estevez, Tom Cruise, Matt Dillon, Patrick Swayze, and Diane Lane. At the time, all were relative unknowns, only to grow to fame in the years following the movie and its eventual cult fandom. *The Outsiders* is credited as the start of the Brat Pack, a riff on the mid-century Rat Pack.

THE OUTSIDERS HOUSE MUSEUM

WHAT: A museum dedicated to the legacy of Francis Ford Coppola's Tulsa-set adaptation of *The Outsiders*

WHERE: 731 N St. Louis Ave., Tulsa

COST: Fee for entry

PRO TIP: Other film sites for *The Outsiders*, in and around Tulsa, include Circle Cinema, the Boston Avenue United Methodist Church, the Admiral Twin Drive-In, and Crutchfield Park, where the Socs attacked Johnny and Pony.

After the movie's release, the "Curtis Brothers House" was abandoned. Until 2016, when musician Danny Boy O'Connor, a fan of both the book and the film, purchased the property to save it from the wrecking ball. He sought to restore the building to its cinematic glory and outfit it with all manner of movie ephemera.

Nowadays, the Outsiders House Museum is a time capsule of cinematic and literary lore. It opened as a nonprofit in 2019, with a ribbon cutting ceremony attended by Hinton. Inside, the home is just as it was on the screen, filled with memorabilia like rare and unseen photos, Coppola's director chair, and hundreds of editions of *The Outsiders* book, in languages from across the globe.

Upon completion of the film, Coppola threw a party in Crutchfield Park, complete with an ice sculpture and carnival games. For his efforts in authentically spotlighting Tulsa, and filming entirely in Oklahoma, the director received a key to the city from the mayor.

Photos courtesy of Phil Clarkin

A MUSEUM FIT FOR TORNADO ALLEY

What's with all the cows?

Considering its location in Tornado Alley, Oklahoma is a fitting location for a major branch of the National Weather Center. It's also a fitting location for a Flying Cow Cafe and a festival dedicated to stormy weather.

The 244,000-square-foot National Weather Center opened in Norman on September 29, 2006, on a 22-acre site at the University of Oklahoma. Ever since, it's operated 24/7/365. The state-of-the-art facility, part education center and part museum, is a joint effort on state, federal, and academic levels, all of whom work to train future meteorologists.

The facility has five functioning floors, plus a sixth-floor observation deck and three extra floors employed solely to contain the 3,200 miles' worth of cable that runs through the building. The server room alone contains

NATIONAL WEATHER CENTER

WHAT: A museum—and annual festival—dedicated to education about Earth's atmosphere

WHERE: 120 David L. Boren Blvd., Norman

COST: Free

PRO TIP: For more *Twister* fandom, visit the Twister the Movie Museum in Wakita, home to autographed memorabilia, debris from the movie, and of course, stuffed cows.

One of the deadliest tornadoes in US history, a mile-wide F5, tore through 38 miles of south Oklahoma City on May 3, 1999, killing 36 people, causing $1 billion in damage, and destroying 1,800 homes.

Photo courtesy of Oklahoma Tourism

1,720 servers and more than two miles of cable beneath the floor. The weather center is also home to the Oklahoma Weather Lab (OWL), a student-run organization that provides weather reports to the university.

Even for those who aren't studying meteorology, Norman's National Weather Center is a fascinating place to visit. Free tours are available, as well as exhibits and a *Twister*-themed Flying Cow Cafe. Dorothy and D.O.T., two iconic props from *Twister*, are in the atrium, where the star attraction is "Science on a Sphere," a massive display of the globe that implements computer and video projections to display animated weather phenomena in real time, all over the world.

A marquee event is the National Weather Festival, which leans into the infamy of Oklahoma's weather with a family-friendly spectacle that attracts thousands of attendees annually in October. The festival features helicopters, weather balloon launches, drone demonstrations, and emergency vehicles, along with organizations like the Storm Prediction Center, local news channels, and of course, the National Weather Center.

OKLAHOMA'S CAMELOT

Who built the stone castle in the woods?

In the 1930s, a local newspaper described a mysterious "Camelot" in the woods in Davis, Oklahoma. Located next to Turner Falls, the largest waterfall in the state, Collings Castle was the vision of Ellsworth Collings, a longtime dean at the University of Oklahoma.

Modest by Camelot standards, the stone structure was built into the hills and contained a main house with three rooms, two living areas, and fireplaces decorated with Oklahoma rose rocks—all interconnected with narrow passageways that seem more like tunnels than halls. There were two adjoining bunkhouses, two outhouses, and a stable, accessed via steps through the trees.

Much of the Collings estate, including artifacts from the castle, have since been moved to the National Cowboy & Western Heritage Museum in Oklahoma City.

Courtesy of Lori Duckworth/Oklahoma Tourism

The reasoning for Collings's ambitions is simple: the "castle" was to serve as a summer home near cabins owned by some of his friends. Considering its proximity to Turner Falls and the swimmable creek and pools it produced, the summer setting was the perfect getaway. Along with help from a "Mr. and Mrs. Parsons," Collings built the castle himself, made mostly from blocks of stone from nearby quarries. The reasoning for the castle facade, specifically, remains a mystery, though historians theorize the stone parapets were merely ornamental, and the narrow windows were an homage to medieval castles in Europe. Collings and his family hosted weekend parties on the castle's outdoor deck, complete with barbecue, while the interior was adorned with stately furnishings like Navajo blankets and oil paintings.

The castle has gone through several hands since Collings's time. A previous owner, Wayne Clemons, was the last to actually live in it—as a caretaker—in the '60s. It was sold to the city of Davis in 1977 and is now overseen by Turner Falls Park.

The castle still stands, though in dilapidated form. A far cry from its opulent origins, no one would confuse this for Camelot nowadays, but rather it's a decrepit stone structure precariously perched on a hillside by a waterfall. Today, it's free to visit with admission to Turner Falls, and many families enjoy exploring the labyrinthine castle.

COLLINGS CASTLE

WHAT: A formerly lavish summer home is now a stone-clad playground by a waterfall.

WHERE: I-35 and US-77, Davis

COST: Entry fee to visit Turner Falls Park

PRO TIP: At 77 feet, Turner Falls is a massive sight to behold. Swimming is no longer permitted at the base of the walls, but visitors can swim in pools along the rest of the creek that flows through the park.

A MANSION OLDER THAN STATEHOOD

OVERHOLSER MANSION

WHAT: Oklahoma's first mansion was an exemplar of Chateauesque in a sea of Prairie-style homes.

WHERE: 405 NW 15th St., Oklahoma City

COST: Tours are available for a fee

PRO TIP: "Christmas at the Overholser" is a seasonal event that allows visitors to tour the house at night, during the holidays, to see the mansion—and every one of its rooms—in luminous grandeur.

Who is the "Father of Oklahoma City"?

Henry Overholser was the kind of entrepreneur made for Oklahoma. Born in Ohio, the businessman arrived in Oklahoma City after the Great Land Run, big plans in tow. Those included erecting businesses practically overnight, being named president of the newly minted Board of Trade, and establishing streetcars and railroads, the latter of which—the St. Louis and Oklahoma City Railroad—linked the brand-new city with Tulsa, St. Louis, and Kansas City. It's no wonder, then, that Overholser was nicknamed the "Father of Oklahoma City." And anyone with such a title needed a mansion befitting the moniker.

By the turn of the century, Oklahoma City's population had tripled. A few years before Oklahoma was declared a state, he and his wife, Anna, purchased three lots in a part of town considered the "country." Nowadays known as downtown-adjacent Heritage Hills, the land was destitute, located more than a mile from the city's economic center.

Overholser commissioned the construction of his mansion in 1903, making it the first of its kind in the territory. Built with Queen Anne and Chateauesque architecture, it was as striking as it was enormous—at 11,000 square feet, the property contained three stories, 20 rooms, and a 4,000-square-foot carriage house.

Photos courtesy of Preservation Oklahoma, Inc.

No expense was spared, either, and the house was decorated with Brussels lace curtains, English carpets, and French stained glass.

The mansion not only laid the foundation for like-minded entrepreneurs to follow but also served as a social hub, host to literary events, dinners, and weddings. The couple gave birth to their daughter, Henry Ione, in the house, and Overholser lived there until his death in 1915. Anna remained in the home until her passing in 1940. After the house was left to their daughter, who was married with no children, the mansion earned protection as a historical landmark.

It joined the National Register of Historic Places in 1970, and then-owner David Jay Perry—widower of Henry Ione—sold everything to the Oklahoma Historical Society. Today, guided tours are offered, along with special events.

Some say that the ghost of Anna Overholser still haunts the mansion, clad in the same lacy white gown that she wore to a 1900 reception for President McKinley.

A ROAD TRIP FOR A FERRIS WHEEL

Why did Santa Monica sell its Ferris wheel on eBay?

Now known as the Wheeler District Ferris Wheel, along the south shore of the Oklahoma River in Oklahoma City, the Americana attraction used to boast a decidedly different backdrop. Some 1,300 miles to the west, it was known as the Pacific Wheel, a 130-foot attraction on the Santa Monica Pier. A star in its own right, the wheel was featured in multiple movies over the course of its time there, including *Iron Man*, *Hancock*, and even *Titanic*.

When Pacific Park decided they wanted to change to a newer wheel, they sold it, literally listing it on eBay. The new Wheeler District, seeking a buzzy new attraction, won a bidding war with $132,400, and the wheel was disassembled, moved to Wichita for refurbishment, and brought to its new home in Oklahoma City. Some $1 million in upgrades later, including 20 shiny new gondolas and 5,400 LEDs, the renamed Wheeler Ferris Wheel was ready to ride again. In July 2016, the attraction was rotating anew.

Considering its location between Los Angeles and Chicago, the two bookends of Route 66, Oklahoma City is a fortuitous locale for a Ferris wheel. Why? Because, much like the Pacific Wheel, Chicago is another city famed for its Ferris wheel legacy. In fact, George Washington Gale Ferris Jr. invented the Ferris wheel and debuted it at the World's Columbian Exposition in

---

The Wheeler Ferris Wheel sits on land that used to be a small airport, the Downtown Airpark, while the neighborhood features streets like Runway Boulevard and Hangar Drive.

Chicago in 1893. Los Angeles's version came much later, in 1996. And now, between the two metropolises, Ferris wheel lore lives on in a new city.

Nowadays, the Wheeler Ferris Wheel continues its legacy. It anchors a sleek new park along the river, complete with hammocks and lawn games, while the Wheeler District continues to develop to the south. It's often used as the backdrop for outdoor festivals, and fittingly, giant letters "OKC" are positioned right in front—a token of its new home.

WHEELER FERRIS WHEEL

WHAT: The iconic Ferris wheel from the Santa Monica Pier was moved and reassembled along the Oklahoma River.

WHERE: 1701 S Western Ave., Oklahoma City

COST: Ticket prices vary for rides, day passes, and season passes

PRO TIP: The Wheeler District is a rapidly developing neighborhood that features new businesses like the Big Friendly brewery, Taco Nation, and Thrown Design & Wine.

Courtesy of Visit OKC

THE "BANDIT QUEEN'S" DEMISE

Courtesy of Oklahoma Historical Society

Who shot Belle Starr in the back?

So named for a curve in the Canadian River, Younger's Bend is a region in eastern Oklahoma that's less famous than it is infamous—thanks to the area's most notorious resident: Belle Starr.

Nicknamed the "Bandit Queen," Starr settled in Younger's Bend after marrying her third husband, Sam Starr, in 1880. The region was rife with ne'er-do-wells, including Jesse James and Cole Younger, whom the bend is reportedly named after, and Starr, in 1886, was quoted in the *Dallas Morning News* as saying, "I am a friend to any brave and gallant outlaw."

Born in Missouri in 1848, Starr was a fearsome outlaw who roamed the plains in velvet skirts, armed with six-shooter artillery. While much is murky about Starr's actions, she was described as an accomplice to her outlawed first husband, Jim Reed, and she provided sanctuary for criminals in Younger's Bend.

Courtesy of Oklahoma Historical Society

The only documented crime that Starr herself was nabbed for was horse theft in 1882.

As a member of the Cherokee Tribe, her third husband, Sam (who she married following a three-week marriage to Bruce Younger), had an allotment of land north of the Canadian River, Younger's Bend, where they lived for almost a decade, including after his death in a shootout in 1886. Tribal leaders didn't want her to remain, considering her lack of Cherokee descent, but she found a loophole by remarrying again—this time to Jim "Bill" July Starr.

Belle remained in Younger's Bend until 1889, when she was mysteriously shot in the back while riding horseback. She was laid to rest by her cabin, and her grave was eventually fortified by a sandstone cover to ward off grave-robbers. It's adorned with a horse-clad headstone that reads, "Shed not for her the bitter tear, Nor give the heart to vain regret, Tis but the casket that lies here, The gem that filled it sparkles yet."

Younger's Bend, and Starr's grave, are on private property, but the public is able to visit the headstone during daytime.

YOUNGER'S BEND

WHAT: The final resting place of outlaw Belle Starr

WHERE: OK-71, Stigler

COST: Free

PRO TIP: A short wooded trail to Starr's gravesite is located along Highway 71, about five miles toward the Lake Eufaula Dam from Porum.

One of Starr's most infamous nicknames was Black Widow, for the fact that all four of her husbands—plus several lovers—met an early demise, from shootouts to mysterious drownings.

OLD JERUSALEM, OLD MOUNTAINS

Courtesy of Oklahoma Tourism

How did a Holy City take shape in the Wichitas?

Amidst the Wichita Mountains, among the oldest mountains on Earth, an ancient-looking community feels more like the Middle East than the Midwest. But despite the fact that the Holy City of the Wichitas resembles Old Jerusalem, it's a relatively recent development with roots in the passion play.

The Passion of the Christ has been the crux of Oklahoma's Holy City since its establishment in 1926. That's when Reverend Anthony Mark Wallock used the rugged backdrop of the Wichita Mountains as an outdoor classroom for his Sunday school. Showcasing the passion play in the arid wilds of the southern Oklahoma mountains, more akin to the environment where Jesus died millennia ago, Wallock began what would become an enduring tradition.

Wallock opened up attendance to the general public, and visitation quickly grew. Less than a decade after his inaugural play, the performance was attracting crowds nearly 6,000

HOLY CITY OF THE WICHITAS

WHAT: The longest-running passion play in the nation takes place in this biblical-looking development in the mountains.

WHERE: 262 Holy City Rd., Lawton

COST: Free (donations accepted)

PRO TIP: The Holy City has a gift shop where visitors can peruse souvenirs and memorabilia, along with a museum filled with artwork and artifacts.

Courtesy of Oklahoma Tourism

strong. With interest rising, so too did the need for infrastructure. While initially plays were performed amidst the natural rusticity of the Wichitas, success paved the way for a full-blown city.

In 1934, the Works Progress Administration established buildings and stages for what is now known as the Holy City of the Wichitas—a direct homage to Old Jerusalem, on 66 acres of land, with structures designed to replicate Pontius Pilate's judgment hall, the Garden of Gethsemane, and more. Perimeter walls, made from local granite, round out the development. Along with other holy features, it laid an accurate backdrop for *The Prince of Peace*, a play that tells of the birth, life, and death of Jesus—a tradition that's continued every year, on Easter Sunday, making it the longest-running passion play in the country.

Nowadays, hundreds of actors and extras appear in the play, and the performance reached an all-time attendance record in 1939, with a whopping 225,000 visitors. The Holy City of the Wichitas is accessible to visitors year round, home to a memorial for the Oklahoma City bombing, a chapel, and Veterans Walkway.

The on-site World Chapel is a popular wedding venue, inspired by Christ Church in Alexandria, Virginia, and complete with murals by artist Irene Malcolm.

WONDERS OF THE BOVINE WORLD

When did Oklahoma become quintessential cattle country?

During the Civil War, the American West was growing—and thundering under the weight of millions of cattle as cowboy-led herds crisscrossed Texas, Oklahoma, and Kansas. The Chisholm Trail, as it became known, was a super highway for cattle and their wranglers, so much so that the 800-mile route has been regarded as one of the "Wonders of the Western World."

While many Texans headed east to fight for the Confederacy, the remaining cattle population ballooned. The stockyard surplus caused the price of cattle to sink, while regions farther north still commanded considerably higher costs per head—in Kansas, a single cow could bring 10 times the value as the same one in Texas.

By 1867, stockyards in Abilene, Kansas, became a mecca for ranchers, where Joseph McCoy encouraged cattle-drivers to bring their herds, and cattle-buyers to buy their beef. Texans got wise to the opportunity, driving their herds—sometimes as large as 10,000 cattle at a time—northward through Oklahoma and into Kansas. Each herd was led by a designated trail boss, and a roster of cowboys equipped with horses and wagons. Along the way, they'd travel 10 miles per day, stopping to rest at watering holes. The trail got its name from Jesse Chisholm,

---

The Wild West outlaw lore from the time is best seen at the Marlow Area Museum in Marlow, an Oklahoma town so named for the Marlow Brothers who were wrongfully accused of stealing cattle.

a part-Cherokee merchant who built a trading post in western Oklahoma City.

Cattle drives reached their apex from 1871 to 1873, with additional runs extended to Kansas towns like Dodge City and Caldwell. The nail in the Chisholm coffin was the Land Run of 1889, which saw the overnight influx of settlers into newly opened Oklahoma Territory, populating the once-wild terrain with farms, private land, and fenced pastures.

For the few short years that the Chisholm Trail thrived, about six million cattle made the trek through Oklahoma Territory, cementing an early reputation as quintessential cattle country. Today, 400 historic trail markers run along the route, with the final one placed in Yukon in 1997.

THE CHISHOLM TRAIL HERITAGE CENTER

WHAT: Cowboy culture and the American West are on full historic display at this museum dedicated to the Chisholm Trail.

WHERE: 2150 Chisholm Trail Pkwy., Duncan

COST: Small fee for entry

PRO TIP: Elsewhere in Duncan, the Trail Ruts at Monument Hill offer the opportunity to see visible remains left by hooves and wagon wheels.

Photos courtesy of Oklahoma Tourism

A DO-OVER FOR THE "WORLD'S GREATEST ATHLETE"

Why did the first Native American Olympian lose his gold medals?

Born in Indian Territory on May 28, 1887, Wa-Tho-Huk was a member of the Sac and Fox Nation, whose name translated to "Bright path the lightning makes as it goes across the sky." It was an apt name for a man who would become the first Native American to win a gold medal at the Olympics, under his more familiar name: Jim Thorpe.

Thorpe didn't get into sports until attending Carlisle Indian Industrial School in Pennsylvania, where he participated in track and field, lacrosse, and baseball. He even tried ballroom dancing, and won the Inter-Collegiate Ballroom Dancing Championship in 1912.

That same year marked the first time that the pentathlon and decathlon were added to the Olympics, taking place in Stockholm. After rigorous training, Thorpe landed a spot on the US Olympics Team, earning gold medals in both categories. In the pentathlon, a five-sport event that included long jump, javelin, 200-meter dash, discus throw, and 1500-meter run, Thorpe

Courtesy of Oklahoma Sports Hall of Fame

tripled the score of his runner-up. The decathlon had 10 events over three days, including shot put, long jump, 100-meter dash, high jump, hurdles, and javelin. He scored 8,413 points, setting a decathlon record that stood for decades. He was the first and only athlete to win both the pentathlon and decathlon.

Thorpe was heralded as the "World's Greatest Athlete." However, once it was discovered that he played professional baseball previously, the Olympics stripped him of his medals. He went on to play baseball, in both the majors and minors, until 1922, and he both played and coached professional football.

The controversy haunted his legacy until his medals were restored in 2022, 69 years after his death by heart attack. Oklahoma honors its star athlete with a Jim Thorpe Museum in Oklahoma City. The two-bedroom home he bought in Yale, Oklahoma, and lived in from 1917 until 1923 is the only home Thorpe ever owned, containing memorabilia from the Native American athlete's life and lore.

Courtesy of Oklahoma Sports Hall of Fame

JIM THORPE MUSEUM

WHAT: A museum-within-a-museum dedicated to the life and legacy of Jim Thorpe

WHERE: 20 S Mickey Mantle Dr., Oklahoma City

COST: Free

PRO TIP: Guided tours are offered at the Jim Thorpe Museum, which is located within the Oklahoma Sports Hall of Fame.

Upon his death, Thorpe's wife sold his remains to the Pennsylvania town of Mauch Chunk, which was subsequently renamed to Jim Thorpe.

LAKE THUNDERBIRD

WHAT: A lake and state park in Norman, said to be one of the dwellings of the Oklahoma Octopus

WHERE: 13101 Alameda Dr., Norman

COST: Fee for parking pass

PRO TIP: The state park features two marinas, campsites, an archery range, picnic shelters, hiking trails, and—if you dare—two swim beaches.

OKLAHOMA'S LOCH NESS MONSTER

Is there really such a thing as the freshwater kraken?

Cryptids, the stuff of urban legends and wild folklore, are a timeworn source of morbid curiosity and mythical adventure. The Loch Ness Monster and Bigfoot are two of the most infamous, while regional creatures across the US include Mothman in West Virginia, the Jersey Devil, and Florida's Skunk Ape. In Oklahoma, in addition to our own Bigfoot mythology, there's one lesser-known cryptid that lurks beneath the surface: the Oklahoma Octopus.

As legend has it, a super-sized freshwater octopus—allegedly the size of a horse—has been documented in Oklahoma lakes like Tenkiller, Thunderbird, and Oologah. Although no footage or physical documentation exists, the eight-limbed cephalopod has been blamed for an unusually high number of drownings and disappearances in the lakes, with several sightings reported over the years. While the likelihood of an octopus living in a lake seems slim (no other species of octopus has been documented doing as such), some have reportedly been seen—at least temporarily—in freshwater, including one found in Arkansas's Lake Conway and another in Oklahoma's Verdigris River.

An indie film, *Oklahoma Octopus: The Freshwater Kraken*, was filmed in Norman and released in 2022.

After appearing in 2007's *Monster Spotter's Guide to North America*, and *A Wizard's Bestiary* that same year, murky mythology began to fuel the folklore flames, with both books describing a large octopus with reddish-brown, leathery skin and a taste for human flesh. Cited as a potential reason for the curiously high number of drownings, and a reason why Native Americans were afraid of the water, it inspired the TV series *Lost Tapes* to stir up further rumors by depicting three swimmers being killed.

Still, despite the Native American lore and unexplained drownings, no firm evidence has ever been uncovered, and interviews with park rangers have been met with confused shrugs. Whether or not a giant, man-eating octopus resides somewhere in Oklahoma's lakes remains to be seen, but the rumors remain lurking beneath the surface.

THE "INDIAN CAPITAL OF THE NATION"

Courtesy of Oklahoma Tourism

How many tribes are headquartered in Anadarko?

Native American history is front-and-center in Oklahoma, a place whose name translates to "Red Earth" in Choctaw, and a state with one of the highest population shares of Indigenous people. This culture is everywhere, but nowhere is it as prominent as in Anadarko, a central Oklahoma town known as the "Indian Capital of the Nation."

NATIONAL HALL OF FAME FOR FAMOUS AMERICAN INDIANS

WHAT: The first Native American hall of fame in the US, featuring dozens of bronze busts in an outdoor garden.

WHERE: 901 E Central Blvd., Anadarko

COST: Free

PRO TIP: Native American murals can be found all over Anadarko, including "Kiowas Moving Camp" at the post office and "Native American Dancer Mural" by Native artist Robert Redbird.

It's a unique distinction for a town where the population is nearly majority Native, and which serves as the headquarters for three tribes: the Delaware Nation, the Apache Tribe, and the Wichita and Affiliated Tribes. This is in addition to local presence from the Caddo Nation, Kiowa Tribe, Comanche Nation, and Fort Sill Apache Tribe, as well as the Bureau of Indian Affairs, a federal agency under the US Department of the Interior, that has a regional office here. The name, Anadarko, comes from a Caddo word, "Na-da-ko," meaning "bumblebee place."

The tribal melting pot stems from centuries of migration. Originally native to Texas, the Na-da-ko tribe were first documented

Photos courtesy of Oklahoma Tourism

by Spanish explorers in 1542. By Texas independence in 1836, they resided along the Trinity River, but clashes with the Republic sent them northward into Indian Territory. Tumult continued for decades, including a brief return to Texas's Brazos River, before white settlers overtook their land. In 1859, they were—once again—relocated to Indian Territory. By 1867, the Na-da-ko tribe had become known as Caddo, and along with the Kadohadacho and Hasinai peoples, formed the Caddo Indian Tribe in 1938.

It's a saga all too familiar, and all too stained on American history. Yet, it's one that is preserved in a town that bears a tribal name, where museums, sculpture gardens, restaurants, and events celebrate that heritage. Today, the Southern Plains Indian Museum and the National Hall of Fame for Famous American Indians (the first of its kind in the US) both reside here, while the annual American Indian Exposition has been held in Anadarko for the better part of a century.

The Wichita Tribal Dance is an annual event held at Wichita Tribal Park in Anadarko, complete with traditional regalia, drums, and gourd dancers.

THE VERY FIRST GIRL SCOUT COOKIE

What was the first Girl Scout Cookie ever made?

Five years after the Girl Scouts were founded as an organization, a simple cookie changed the world—and it all started in the eastern Oklahoma town of Muskogee.

The year was 1917, when Marion D. Brown organized the town's first Girl Scouts, the Mistletoe Troop. Their first meeting was held bright and early on October 17 of that year, when the troop was divvied into platoons with captains, and they all taught themselves US history, Scout laws, and other activities. One of their earlier endeavors was raising funds for Oklahoma soldiers overseas, which they did by selling cookies and popcorn balls out of the Muskogee Central High School cafeteria.

Courtesy of Three Rivers Museum

A far cry from the iconic cookie lineup so widely known today, their first batch was just a simple sugar cookie, without any bells or whistles, since they were all made from scratch out of home kitchens, either by Girl Scouts themselves or their relatives. It was nothing fancy, but the school sale was such a success that word began to spread to other troops across the country, who began their own home-baked traditions. In 1922, *American Girl* magazine printed a recipe for said sugar cookies, along with a gentle nudge that they could be sold door-to-door to raise money.

THREE RIVERS MUSEUM

WHAT: A Muskogee museum with a Girl Scout statue and exhibits

WHERE: 220 Elgin St., Muskogee

COST: Fee for entry

PRO TIP: A Girl Scout statue, *A Promise to Keep*, was dedicated outside of the museum in 2008—complete with a stack of cookie boxes, naturally.

It remained a homespun endeavor until 1934, when troops in Philadelphia began selling the first batches made in a commercial kitchen, thus expanding their capacity and, eventually, their varieties. Thin Mints first emerged, initially as Cooky-Mints, in 1939, followed swiftly by a sandwich cookie and a shortbread. Thin Mints, though, remain the top seller. Some, like Thin Mints, have endured, while others—like Kookaburras and Golden Yangles—have come and gone.

But as the originator of the tradition, selling cookies to raise funds, Muskogee's Mistletoe Troop can lay claim to one of the sweetest entrepreneurial innovations in American history.

Aside from requisites, like Thin Mints, Girl Scout cookies vary regionally, but some of the staples available in Oklahoma include Girl Scout S'mores, Lemon-Ups, and brownie-inspired Adventurefuls.

MAIN STREET OIL WELL

WHAT: Located in the middle of Main Street, it's the only oil well of its kind in the world.

WHERE: 800-898 W Main St., Barnsdall

COST: Free

PRO TIP: Barnsdall's Bigheart Museum contains artifacts and exhibits detailing the town's history, including its role in the oil industry.

MAIN STREET OIL WELL, USA

Why did Barnsdall's tiny well stop pumping?

Oil wells are not a rare sight in Oklahoma. In fact, the Oklahoma State Capitol building, in Oklahoma City, holds the distinction as the only capitol complex in the world to be surrounded by active oil wells. Across the state, huge drilling machines can be seen extracting petroleum oil from beneath Earth's surface. But in the town of Barnsdall, there's one oil well unlike any other—notable for the fact that it's as tiny as the town's population, and the only one in the world to be located in the middle of an active street.

Essentially a miniature version of typical oil wells, Barnsdall's Main Street version is barely eight feet tall, surrounded by a modest fence in the center of the road, which splits to go around it. It was dug in 1914, by the Indian Territory Illuminating Oil Company, to anticipate the oil boom sweeping the state. The industry became so prosperous that the town changed from its original name, Bigheart, to Barnsdall, in honor of oil tycoon Theodore Newton Barnsdall.

Nicknamed the "King of Hollywood," Clark Gable lived in Barnsdall for years, and his shotgun house on West Walnut Street still stands today.

Courtesy of Oklahoma Historical Society

The tiny Main Street well pumped oil for years, until the '60s, due to the depletion of its reservoir. Although a sign on the fence declared that it could begin pumping again at any moment, it's remained dormant ever since. Despite its lack of oil extraction, the diminutive well has become an in-the-know roadside attraction, for the unique fact that—in a state saturated with oil rigs—it's in a league entirely its own. So much so that it was added to the National Register of Historic Places in 1997.

ALLEYWAY ART GALLERY

How did graffiti change Oklahoma City's art scene forever?

In recent years, Oklahoma City has emerged as an epicenter of street art, consistently topping national polls for public art. And much of that success stems from a mural initiative launched in 2015.

That's when Oklahoma City's Plaza District created the nonprofit Oklahoma Mural Syndicate to fund the Plaza Walls. Similar, in theory, to the famed Wynwood Walls in Miami, where alleyway murals transformed a derelict warehouse district into a hotbed of galleries and activations, the Plaza Walls were envisioned as a rotating outdoor gallery, featuring murals in an alley behind storefronts along the neighborhood's main drag.

Courtesy of Ryan Magnani

With approval from the Oklahoma City Arts and Urban Design Commissions, and a goal to support and highlight the local artist community, the Walls transformed an overlooked space into the city's most dynamic gallery. Since its inception, the Walls have grown in size and scope, featuring well over 100 murals from artists across the country and a dedicated Plaza Walls storefront stocked with artist-made merchandise.

The Plaza Walls marked the first area in the city to feature legally permitted graffiti, displayed along Indiana Avenue. The art expanded, manifesting in various forms along 16th Street, Indiana Avenue, and especially through the alley that winds behind businesses like Bad Granny's Bazaar and Dig It Boutique. Murals rotate regularly, providing fresh opportunities for artists—emerging, established, and everywhere in between—to imprint themselves upon a living public gallery.

The Plaza Walls are freely accessible 24/7/365, featuring larger-than-life murals that run the gamut in terms of style, expression, and inspiration.

PLAZA WALLS

WHAT: Rotating artist murals line the alleys behind Oklahoma City's Plaza District.

WHERE: 1745 NW 16th St., Oklahoma City

COST: Free

PRO TIP: Grab a drink at RadBar, a graffiti-filled bar owned by Kris Kanaly, one of the founding members of the Oklahoma Mural Syndicate.

The Plaza District hosts regular "Live on the Plaza" street festivals throughout the year, offering family-friendly activities and music, along with an apt opportunity to view the public art.

OKLAHOMA'S NUTTIEST FOOD FESTIVAL

Courtesy of Pie Junkie

How long have pecans been grown in Oklahoma?

If there's one native ingredient that really typifies Oklahoma food, it's the humble pecan. While often associated with more of the Deep South and Southwest (it's the state nut in places like Alabama and Louisiana), Oklahoma is one of the top pecan-producing states in the nation, with recent annual crops exceeding 23 million pounds during pecan season in the fall.

Native Americans have harvested the crops for centuries, before Spanish explorers "discovered" them in the 1500s. US farmers began planting pecan seeds in the 1700s, and across the state today, pecans are grown in 60 out of 77 counties, with 75 percent of production coming from native trees—making Oklahoma second in the nation for native pecan production (as opposed to non-native, or cultivated, pecans). Technically drupes, rather than nuts, pecans are Oklahoma's largest fruit tree crop, in the same family as cherries, olives, and coconuts. All those drupes make for a booming industry: a recent US Census of Agriculture found more than 2,044 pecan farms in Oklahoma, across more than 100,000 acres.

Snag a slice of pecan pie at Oklahoma City's Pie Junkie, an award-winning bakery renowned for both classic and contemporary flavors.

What makes Oklahoma so ripe for pecans? It's the perfect combination of sunlight, rich soil, and just enough rainfall, all of which allow for fertile farms—most situated along creeks and rivers—to harvest hundreds of pounds per acre annually. Of the hundreds of varieties of pecans, Oklahoma is unique in that numerous species have been tested and named by the Oklahoma Agricultural Experiment Station, including many after Native tribes like Choctaw, Kiowa, and Oconee.

OKMULGEE PECAN FESTIVAL

WHAT: A decades-old festival celebrating Okmulgee's pecan history and heritage

WHERE: Fairgrounds Rd., Okmulgee (Claude Cox Omniplex)

COST: Free

PRO TIP: A new addition to the Pecan Festival is a beard and mustache contest, which is open to kids who want to craft their own fake facial hair.

Pecan pie is part of the Oklahoma State Meal, and pecan wood stokes the flames for many local barbecue spots. Pecans also get their own spotlight at the annual Okmulgee Pecan Festival, a decades-old community event celebrating one of the state's star crops, with carnival-style games, a car show, baking contests, and of course, pecans aplenty.

Courtesy of Pie Junkie

OKLAHOMA'S OLDEST TOWN IS ELECTRIFYING

What inspired Vinita to host its own "Great White Way"?

Eighteen years before statehood, a town in northeast Oklahoma illuminated the way. An enduring stopover on Route 66 and home to the oldest continuously operating restaurant on the Mother Road (Clanton's Cafe), Vinita holds the dual distinction of being the oldest incorporated town in Oklahoma and the first to have electricity, nearly two decades before the territory became a state.

EASTERN TRAILS MUSEUM

WHAT: A local history museum detailing Vinita's Native American heritage, pop culture, electricity, and more

WHERE: 215 W Illinois Ave., Vinita

COST: Free

PRO TIP: The museum is just a few blocks from Clanton's Cafe, the oldest continuously operating restaurant on Route 66, which is known for its chicken-fried steak.

The community was established in 1871 by Cherokee leader Elias C. Boudinot, who, like many Native Americans, had been forcibly moved to Indian Territory to start a new life. Vinita was initially named Downingville but later renamed in honor of his friend, sculptress Lavinia "Vinnie" Ellen Ream Hoxie.

Vinita, in its early heyday, was a boom town. Thanks to its location on several developing routes and railways, it quickly became one of the most populous towns in the young state, with new businesses—like the historic Center Theatre—to meet the growing demand. It was also, notably, the first town in Oklahoma to get electricity, which helped provide infrastructure for the growing community.

Courtesy of Eastern Trails Museum

That's courtesy of the Vinita Electric Light, Ice, and Power Company, which was chartered with establishing electric service in Indian Territory way back in 1889. Later renamed Public Service Company of Oklahoma (PSO), it's still around today and boasts more than half a million customers throughout the state, while generating a capacity of 4,269 megawatts. To celebrate the advent of widespread electricity in Oklahoma, locals held an event in the summer of 1930, called the Great White Way, after the bright lights of Broadway in New York, and a similar celebration held there a few years prior. For the first time, electricity meant that lights could keep businesses booming after dark and provide new opportunities for commerce and entertainment.

A noted sculptor, Vinnie Ream was the first woman commissioned to make art for the US government: a sculpture of Abraham Lincoln in the Capitol Rotunda in 1871.

THE COW-CHIP-THROWING CAPITAL

How did manure become a sport?

Cow manure has long been a resource for soil enrichment, but in the Oklahoma panhandle, it's fodder for sport. In the early days of settlement, pioneers had to find other resources for fuel on the mostly treeless plains. Naturally, they turned to what resources they had at their disposal: dried piles of cow manure, otherwise known as cow chips.

By scooping up these dried, disc-shaped piles, which are a reliable source of odorless fuel, settlers began to make sport out of tossing them into their wagons. Over time, what began as a necessary resource for heating homes and fueling stoves became a game—with locals aiming for accuracy and distance with their cow chip tosses. In the town of Beaver, specifically, tossing cow chips became such a hallmark tradition that the town held the world's first sanctioned cow-chip-throwing contest in 1970.

Courtesy of Oklahoma Historical Society

Ever since, folks flock from far and wide to hurl cow chips as part of the World Cow Chip Throwing Contest, a marquee event connected to the Beaver County Free Fair. Along with a carnival, talent show, entertainment, chili cook-off, and parade (complete with a 10-foot-tall beaver statue holding a super-sized cow chip), the contest is held in August. Locals, along with VIP guests, like celebrities and politicians, are welcome to try their hand at throwing cow chips the farthest.

A recent world record-holder for farthest throw in the cow chip contest, Oklahoman Drew Russell hurled his dung a remarkable 188 feet and six inches.

Courtesy of Oklahoma Historical Society

WORLD COW CHIP THROWING CONTEST

WHAT: An annual cow chip competition anchors the Beaver County Free Fair, complete with a parade, entertainment, music, talent show, and more.

WHERE: 1107 Douglas Ave., Beaver

COST: Free to attend

PRO TIP: One of the popular snacks to try at the fair is cow chip cookies, which are a kind of chocolate chip cookie baked to resemble you-know-what.

After initially using bison chips, settlers turned to a more readily available resource, cow chips. When dried, cow dung emits no odor, gives off a bright flame, and burns hot with no soot—making it ideal fuel for warming homes and stoves on the harsh plains.

A HIPPOPOTAMUS FOR CHRISTMAS

Did the zoo help invent a holiday song?

From "Feliz Navidad" to "Jingle Bell Rock," classic Christmas songs have brought holiday cheer for generations. One of the most peculiar Christmas songs, though, got its start in an equally peculiar place: at the Oklahoma City Zoo.

"I Want a Hippopotamus for Christmas," released in 1953, was recorded by Gayla Peevey, a 10-year-old resident of Oklahoma City. Prior to her big break, when Columbia Records caught wind of the musical prodigy, Peevey sang on a local radio broadcast and at indie Oklahoma events like the Sooner Shindig. Television stints began picking up in 1953, prompting the family to relocate to California, before recording her hit song—written by John Rox—in New York City.

OKLAHOMA CITY ZOO

WHAT: A 130-acre zoo and botanical garden, home to more than 2,000 animals in Oklahoma City's Adventure District

WHERE: 2000 Remington Pl., Oklahoma City

COST: Fee for entry

PRO TIP: Though there aren't currently any hippos at the zoo, the newest addition is Expedition Africa, a 12-acre habitat with animals like hyenas, lemurs, cheetahs, giraffes, and zebras.

Upon its release, "I Want a Hippopotamus for Christmas" peaked at 23 on the Billboard Music Chart and sold more than 300,000 copies. Peevey's star was ascending, too, with

"I Want a Hippopotamus for Christmas" has become a holiday staple, covered by the likes of the Jonas Brothers, LeAnn Rimes, and Kacey Musgraves.

appearances on national programs like the *Ed Sullivan Show*. Riding the wave of popularity, Peevey's hometown became inspired by her and her song—the Oklahoma City Zoo, which did not have a hippopotamus, started a campaign to get one for Peevey.

Oklahoma newspapers began promoting the campaign and encouraged readers to donate dimes and quarters to the Peevey-inspired hippo fund. The campaign lived up to the song and was successful in purchasing a baby hippo, named Matilda, for Peevey in 1953. She donated the hippo to the zoo on Christmas Eve of that year, fulfilling the wish she had been singing about.

Matilda lived at the Oklahoma City Zoo for 45 years, and Peevey—now nicknamed Oklahoma's "Queen of Christmas"—regularly returns to the zoo for Christmas appearances and performances. In honor of Peevey's legacy, the zoo unveiled a life-sized bronze sculpture of the young singer and baby Matilda, titled *Gayla's Hippo Hero*.

Photos courtesy of Oklahoma City Zoo

CALF FRY COUNTRY

How did fried testicles become an Oklahoma food tradition?

WORLD'S LARGEST CALF FRY FESTIVAL & COOK-OFF

WHAT: Calf fries take center stage at this long-running annual food festival in Vinita.

WHERE: Craig County Fairgrounds, 915 E Apperson Rd., Vinita

COST: Fee for entry

PRO TIP: Not keen on eating fried testicles? The festival also serves a wide array of other comfort foods, like breads, salsas, and cobblers.

Here in cattle country, comfort food comes in many forms, from chicken-fried steak and crispy okra to pecan pie and onion burgers. One such comfort, though, is an acquired taste that stems from cowboys, ranchers, and a fearless sense of scrappy cookery. Calf fries, otherwise known as fried bull testicles or Rocky Mountain oysters, are a longtime staple in Oklahoma that have become such a fixture that they've emerged on menus and headlined food festivals.

Much like onion burgers, calf fries first emerged as ranchers sought to utilize every part of the animal, in order to eat cheaply and gain protein. While sometimes grilled or baked, frying became the most commonplace method (and likely the most palatable), thus earning the inoffensive moniker "calf fries."

A culinary tradition dating back to ancient Rome, eating offal and organ meats—like bull testicles—was said to improve the health of the corresponding human organs. Thus, calf fries are said to be an aphrodisiac.

Courtesy of Visit OKC/Cattlemen's Steakhouse

Though the days of resourceful ranch cooking have largely ebbed, calf fries—along with similar preparations, like lamb fries—remain a "when in Rome"-style Oklahoma delicacy. Calf fries are a requisite at Clanton's Cafe in Vinita, the oldest continuously operating restaurant on Route 66. And at Cattlemen's Steakhouse, the oldest restaurant in Oklahoma City, lamb fries are the testicles du jour, dredged in flour and deep-fried, chosen for their consistency over bull testicles.

They've become such a rite of passage that they've inspired more than one calf fry festival, including the annual Tumbleweed calf fry musical and food festival in Stillwater, and the World's Largest Calf Fry Festival & Cook-Off in Vinita. The latter has been held since 1979 and has grown to include entertainment, rides, arts and crafts, and of course, plenty of calf fries to sample. In fact, the festival serves an average of 2,000 pounds of calf fries each year, including those served by teams competing in the cook-off, as determined by local celebrity judges.

SOURCES

Oklahoma's Own John Wilkes Booth
okhistory.org/publications/enc/entry?entry=BO016
okhauntedhouses.com/real-haunt/garfield-furniture--grand-avenue-hotel.html
downtownenidhistory.com/205-s-grand/205-s-grand-enid-ok
enidnews.com/news/local_news/a-deathbed-claim/article_7d7c3983-4c54-505c-b688-ea15d37c5f5b.html
amberandchaos.net/?p=215

The Nation's Capital of All-Black Towns
humanities.utulsa.edu/oklahoma-home-historically-black-towns-u-s-state
okhistory.org/publications/enc/entry.php?entry=AL009#:~:text=Towns%20that%20still%20survive%20are,renowned%20of%20these%20was%20Boley.
ocpathink.org/post/independent-journalism/slave-owning-past-remains-problem-for-choctaws#:~:text=The%20tribe's%20argument%20has%20drawn,and%20Muscogee%20(Creek)%20nations.
tulsaworld.com/news/local/history/photos-the-13-historic-all-black-towns-that-remain-in-oklahoma/collection_7d1d7b5d-662c-54a0-a072-bc560fdf6756.html
koco.com/article/oklahoma-boley-all-black-town-history/42736603
travelok.com/listings/view.profile/id.675
boleytours.com

Wealth, Infamy, and the FBI
okhistory.org/publications/enc/entry.php?entry=OS001
legendsofamerica.com/black-dog-trail-treasure
history.com/news/osage-murders-reign-terror-husbands-guardians
okhistory.org/publications/enc/entry.php?entry=OS005#:~:text=Estimates%20vary%2C%20but%20approximately%20twenty,deaths%20during%20the%20early%201920s.
missourilife.com/the-osage-nation-today/
history.com/news/the-fbis-first-big-case-the-osage-murders
osageculture.com/culture/museum
travelok.com/articles/osage-county-native-american-history-culture

The Real Man Behind *Oklahoma!*
okhistory.org/learn/musical1#:~:text=In%201931%20Lynn%20Riggs%20published,before%20Oklahoma%20became%20a%20state.
claremoremoh.org
rodgersandhammerstein.com
breakingcharacter.com/rodgers-and-hammersteins-oklahoma-laurence-maslon/
thislandpress.com/2014/04/30/broadways-forgotten-man

The Action Figure Museum That Saved a Town
toyandactionfiguremuseum.com/about-us
travelok.com/listings/view.profile/id.7991
roadsideamerica.com/story/14149
oklahoman.com/story/lifestyle/2021/04/12/relive-some-childhood-memories-toy-museum-pauls-valley-oklahoma/7104949002
oklahoman.com/story/news/2006/05/24/drawing-interestbrmuseum-celebrates-work-of-oklahoma-cartoonists/61882383007

America's Most Underrated Burger
eater.com/23561167/oklahoma-onion-burger-el-reno-roberts-grill-sids-diner-johnnies-tuckers#:~:text=Legend%20has%20it%20that%20the,in%20his%20five%2Dcent%20burgers.
foodandwine.com/news/oklahoma-onion-burger-national-treasure
tastingtable.com/1054284/the-humble-origins-of-oklahomas-onion-burger
cowboysindians.com/2017/09/taste-of-the-west-the-oklahoma-fried-onion-burger
elrenoburgerday.com
travelok.com/listings/view.profile/id.18163#:~:text=Attend%20the%20Fried%20Onion%20Burger,hamburger%2C%20weighing%20over%20850%20lbs.

95% of an Apache Icon's Grave
roadsideamerica.com/tip/16666
http://blogoklahoma.us/place/389/comanche/geronimo-grave-marker
npr.org/2009/03/09/101626709/mystery-of-the-bones-geronimos-missing-skull
okhistory.org/publications/enc/entry?entry=GE009
campingandtrekking.com/geronimos-gravesite-on-fort-sill-oklahoma/#:~:text=His%20grave%20is%20located%20on,the%20Fort%20Sill%20Visitor%20Center.
travelok.com/listings/view.profile/id.29308
ctinsider.com/news/article/yale-secret-society-steal-famous-apache-leader-s-18085455.php

A Standout Moment in the Sit-In Movement
kfor.com/news/local/a-1958-drug-store-sit-in-helped-shape-civil-rights-in-okc

freedomcenterokc.org
freedomcenterokc.org/news/a-monument-in-bronze-for-a-teacher
zinnedproject.org/news/tdih/katz-drug-store-sit-ins
okhistory.org/publications/enc/entry.php?entry=LU005
history.com/topics/black-history/civil-rights-movement
britannica.com/event/sit-in-movement
lowellmilkencenter.org/programs/projects/view/clara-luper-a-leader-in-desegregations-sit-in-movement/hero

How a Star Architect Faded into a Footnote
okhistory.org/publications/enc/entry?entry=GO001
nytimes.com/2018/09/10/t-magazine/bruce-goff-architecture-midwest.html
papercitymag.com/home-design/bruce-goff-controversial-great-american-architect-hidden-sides
okcmod.com/2015/07/why-did-henry-kamphoefner-and-crew-leave-ou
re-thinkingthefuture.com/know-your-architects/bruce-goff-15-iconic-projects
architecturaldigest.com/story/tulsa-art-deco-architecture

The Center of the Universe
atlasobscura.com/places/the-center-of-the-universe-tulsa-oklahoma
travelok.com/listings/view.profile/id.19397
downtowntulsa.com/about/programs-and-initiatives/recentertheuniverse
publicradiotulsa.org/local-regional/2022-12-13/proposed-plans-for-center-of-the-universe-unveiled
tulsapeople.com/city-desk/the-center-of-the-universe/article_e14638d8-0273-11eb-b788-7f81459d85d2.html

A Castle Fit for a Governor
lake-murray.org/tucker-tower
wanderwisdom.com/travel-destinations/TuckersTower
travelok.com/state-parks/lake-murray-state-park
lakemurrayoklahoma.com/camping-rv-parks#:~:text=The%20ten%20campgrounds%20on%20Lake,many%20sites%20on%20the%20shoreline.
travelok.com/listings/view.profile/id.18224#:~:text=Located%20within%20Oklahoma's%20largest%20state,park%20office%20and%20fishing%20pier.
okhistory.org/publications/enc/entry?entry=LA008
oklahoman.com/story/news/2013/09/01/updated-tucker-tower-an-old-oklahoma-landmark-open-for-labor-day-at-lake-murray/60886211007/#:~:text=Tucker%20Tower%2C%20a%2078%2Dyear,lake%20area%20starting%20in%201933.
onlineonly.christies.com/s/deep-impact-lunar-rare-meteorites/complete-slice-oldest-meteorite-earth-lake-murray-8/82791

The Palace That Oil Built
travelok.com/articles/the-marland-mansion-ponca-citys-palace-on-the-prairie
marlandmansion.com
travelok.com/listings/view.profile/id.4836
yourponcacity.com/articles/marland-mansion-tour/19933
marlandgrandhome.com

Stop and Smell the Rose Rocks
cityofnoble.org/rose-rock-festival
ou.edu/ogs/generalinterest/rose_rocks#:~:text=History%20and%20Lore,House%20of%20Representatives%20in%201983.
okhistory.org/publications/enc/entry.php?entry=RO030
normantranscript.com/news/noble-holds-tight-to-rose-rock-capital-title/article_7ba5b060-fd9f-11ed-86c4-e727a6ca6d54.html
nobleok.org/rose-rock-music-festival
treewizardworkshop.com

The Smile Seen around the World
eskimojoes.com
tulsaworld.com/archive/juke-joint-not-just-suds-eskimo-joes-turns-35-into-legend/article_d868092d-2d81-5d47-9c47-fc9c18daaca4.html

The Mini Mosque That Shaped a City
visittulsa.com/plan-your-visit/districts/downtown-tulsa/blue-dome-district
bluedomedistrict.com
atlasobscura.com/places/blue-dome-tulsa
hmdb.org/m.asp?m=142265
nps.gov/articles/route-66-1926-1945.htm

The Bermuda Triangle of the Plains
travelok.com/articles/oklahomas-spooky-urban-legends
onlyinyourstate.com/oklahoma/sinister-beaver-dunes-park-ok
jahernandez.com/posts/shamans-portal-in-oklahoma
travelok.com/listings/view.profile/id.418
weathergeeks.org/green-lightning
puzzleboxhorror.com/shamans-portal-of-beaver-dunes-park-oklahoma

The Dust Bowl Forest
atlasobscura.com/places/parallel-forest
thrillist.com/travel/nation/visit-parallel-for-

est-oklahoma
okhistory.org/learn/depression2
britannica.com/place/Dust-Bowl
405magazine.com/pictures-from-the-parallel-forest/#:~:text=In%20the%20spring%20of%201912,verge%20of%20a%20changing%20era.

A Honky-Tonk with History
cainsballroom.com
southernliving.com/cains-ballroom-oklahoma-7107564
travelok.com/music-trail/venues/cain-s-ballroom
cainsballroom.com/cains-ballroom-the-history-behind-tulsas-historic-music-venue
cainsballroom.com/event/bob-wills-texas-playboys-saturday/cains-ballroom/tulsa--oklahoma
countrymusichalloffame.org/hall-of-fame/bob-wills
sfae.com/Artists/Lynn-Goldsmith/Sid-Vicious-Cain-s-Ballroom-Tulsa-OK-1978
atlasobscura.com/places/cains-ballroom

The Lost National Park
home.nps.gov/chic/index.htm
travelok.com/listings/view.profile/id.1349
okhistory.org/publications/enc/entry?entry=CH035
npr.org/2016/08/09/489190190/in-oklahoma-a-national-park-that-got-demoted
travelandleisure.com/chicksaw-recreation-area-oklahoma-indigenous-land-8412036

The Greatest Cemetery on Earth
atlasobscura.com/places/showmen-s-rest
travelok.com/listings/view.profile/id.5187
atlasobscura.com/articles/circus-cemetery-hugo-oklahoma
onlyinyourstate.com/oklahoma/circus-cemetery-ok
circusdiner.com/about.html

A "Mini" World Trade Center
atlasobscura.com/places/bok-tower
mcalesternews.com/news/local_news/cathey-oklahoma-s-little-cousin-to-the-twin-towers/article_7949ffaf-3be3-5854-a412-8771aca434ce.html
weburbanist.com/2016/05/10/14-world-trade-center-tulsas-half-sized-untwinned-tower
tulsa.tours/tulsa-tunnel-tour

The Mother of the Mother Road
lucillesroadhouse.com
travelok.com/listings/view.profile/id.14568
roadsideamerica.com/tip/3094
legendsofamerica.com/hydro-oklahoma/
travelok.com/listings/view.profile/id.14568#:~:text=Built%20in%201929%20by%20Carl,the%20business%20for%2060%20years.

Black Wall Street
greenwoodrising.org
localprojects.com/work/museums-attractions/greenwood-rising
tulsahistory.org/exhibit/1921-tulsa-race-massacre
memory.loc.gov/diglib/legacies/loc.afc.afc-legacies.200003712/#:~:text=The%20first%20oil%20was%20struck,1882%20to%2072%2C000%20in%201920.

The Stolen State Capital
publishingmuseum.org/explore/history
okhistory.org/sites/territorialmuseum
okterritorialmuseum.org/ABOUT.html
digitalprairieok.net/state-capital-moves/#:~:text=Governor%20Charles%20Haskell%20called%20a,Shawnee%20last%20(8%2C402%20votes).
okhistory.org/learn/publishingmuseum
okhistory.org/learn/capitol1#:~:text=With%20this%20in%20mind%2C%20cities,with%2050%2C000%20votes%20over%20Guthrie.
cityofguthrie.com/97/Historic-Preservation

Ancient Peaks
fws.gov/refuge/wichita-mountains
travelok.com/listings/view.profile/id.8525
okhistory.org/publications/enc/entry?entry=WI003
blogoklahoma.us/place/377/comanche/wichita-mountains-wildlife-refuge
okhistory.org/publications/enc/entry?entry=WI002#:~:text=The%20Wichita%20Mountains%20are%20geologically,heights%20greater%20than%20at%20present.
oklahoman.com/story/news/1984/04/15/ancient-plains-life-unraveled/62806803007
samnoblemuseum.ou.edu/common-fossils-of-oklahoma/paleocommunities/marine-communities/ordovician-communities

Alligators on the Prairie
wildlifedepartment.com/hunting/wma/southeast/red-slough-wma
fs.usda.gov/detail/ouachita/landmanagement/?cid=STELPRDB5090471
travelok.com/listings/view.profile/id.6279
beaversbendcabincountry.com/parks/forests-wetlands/red-slough
worldpopulationreview.com/state-rankings/alligators-by-state

The Tree That Inspired Hope
memorialmuseum.com
memorialmuseum.com/experience/the-survivor-tree
memorialmuseum.com/experience/the-survivor-tree/the-survivor-tree-then
rtectreecare.com/survivor-tree
oklahoman.com/story/news/local/oklahoma-city/2017/04/19/oklahoma-citys-survivor-tree-seedlings-have-spread-across-the-nation/60605143007
scissortailpark.org/survivor-tree-clone-transplanted-at-scissortail-park

A Haunted Mansion
http://stonelioninn.com/index.html
travelok.com/listings/view.profile/id.7271
hauntedrooms.com/oklahoma/haunted-places/haunted-hotels/stone-lion-inn-guthrie
chrie.org/assets/docs/JHTC-case-notes/JHTC-vol-5/JHTC_Vol5Issue2-Soulek_case.pdf

The Skyscraper That Lava Built
travelok.com/state-parks/black-mesa-state-park-nature-preserve
nature.org/en-us/get-involved/how-to-help/places-we-protect/black-mesa-preserve/
hipcamp.com/en-US/p/united-states/oklahoma/state-park/black-mesa/all
travelok.com/listings/view.profile/id.18259
reddit.com/r/oklahoma/comments/qptaie/the_trail_up_to_black_mesa_the_highest_point_in

A Whale on Route 66
travelok.com/listings/view.profile/id.653
roadsideamerica.com/story/14307
wanderwisdom.com/travel-destinations/The-Catoosa-Blue-Whale-A-Whale-of-a-Tale
waymarking.com/waymarks/WMRAJ6_Natures_Acres_Defunct_Amusement_Park_Catoosa_Oklahoma_USA

Concrete Folk Art
travelok.com/listings/view.profile/id.13179
nps.gov/places/ed-galloways-totem-pole-park.htm
legendsofamerica.com/ok-totempolepark/#:~:text=Ed%20Galloway%20built%20the%20totem,each%20representing%20a%20different%20tribe.
\rchs1.org/totem-pole-park

Deep-Fried History at Oklahoma's Oldest Bar
eischensbar.com
travelok.com/listings/view.profile/id.2505
savingplaces.org/stories/eischens-bar-in-okarche-oklahoma
atlasobscura.com/places/eischens-bar
eater.com/23171858/best-fried-chicken-restaurants-america

The Space Cowboy of the Great Plains
buckatomson66.com
travelok.com/listings/view.profile/id.26889
roadsideamerica.com/story/64851
theroute-66.com/muffler-men-on-route-66.html

A House Fit for a Flintstone
cavehousetulsa.com
travelok.com/listings/view.profile/id.22342
atlasobscura.com/places/cave-house-tulsa
kfor.com/news/great-state/the-current-owner-of-tulsas-cave-house-has-the-key-to-a-colorful-history
wanderwisdom.com/travel-destinations/TulsaCaveHouse

The Oklahoma Walk of Fame
circlecinema.org/walk-of-fame
fox23.com/news/circle-cinema-celebrates-95th-birthday-unveils-walk-of-fame-inductees/article_bab187ee-2373-11ee-90c8-03b43191cff5.html
salina.com/story/entertainment/movies/2017/04/24/circle-cinema-s-walk-fame/20565939007
circlecinema.org/ccff

Fine Dining in the Forest
livingkitchenfarm.com
travelok.com/listings/view.profile/id.11599
oklahomatoday.com/online-exclusive/editors-blog/bucket-list-road-living-kitchen-farm-and-dairy
edibletulsa.ediblecommunities.com/eat/paradise-porch-living-kitchen-farm-table-dinners

A Cobblestone Oasis for Outlaws
medicinepark.com
travelok.com/medicine_park
okhistory.org/publications/enc/entry?entry=ME006
onlyinyourstate.com/oklahoma/small-town-with-unique-history-ok/
parenthoodandpassports.com/things-to-do-in-medicine-park-oklahoma/
okhistory.org/publications/enc/entry?entry=CA045#:~:text=Through%20the%201910s%20and%201920s,dozen%20buildings%20on%20the%20refuge.

A Ghostly Mound
kfor.com/news/great-state/a-shocking-find-on-the-summit-of-ghost-mound
kgou.org/show/how-curious/2021-10-27/how-curious-what-oklahoma-mound-inspired-an-h-p-lovecraft-story
swoknews.com/styles/the-legends-of-ghost-mound-told/article_a5a7ef81-ee41-5c13-986e-230c4d85b9dc.html
facebook.com/pages/Hinton%20Historical%20Museum/370093769727390

America's Most Toxic Ghost Town
oklahoman.com/story/news/2023/10/30/how-picher-oklahoma-became-americas-most-toxic-ghost-town/70992699007
quirkytravelguy.com/visiting-picher-oklahoma-ghost-town-toxic-waste
okhistory.org/publications/enc/entry?entry=PI002

The Sooner State Sasquatch
okcfox.com/news/local/bigfoot-sighting-colorado-sasquatch-native-oklahoma-bigfoot-research-organization-brian-terrell-cryptid-strange
kjrh.com/news/positively-oklahoma/bigfoot-is-scaring-up-tourism-dollars-for-oklahoma
scrippsnews.com/stories/remote-oklahoma-town-has-become-hub-for-bigfoot-believers
honobiabigfoot.com/festival
oklahoman.com/story/news/2023/12/22/oklahomas-honobia-bigfoot-festival-in-question-what-to-know/71998806007/
sites.google.com/site/nativeokbigfoot-research/home
qcnews.com/news/national-news/bigfoot-sightings-which-states-have-the-most/#:~:text=According%20to%20the%20Bigfoot%20Field,been%20708%20%E2%80%9Ccredible%E2%80%9D%20sightings.
visitcalifornia.com/road-trips/bigfoot-scenic-byway
travelok.com/listings/view.profile/id.21807

Modernist Architecture Meets Televangelism
atlasobscura.com/places/abundant-life-building
gateway.okhistory.org/ark:/67531/metadc1472295
abandonedok.com/abundant-life-building/
apnews.com/general-news-df6ea8f00d-fa43851fbcc08a64e22cca#:~:text=The%20building%20was%20originally%20constructed,been%20vacant%20since%20the%201980s
oru.edu/life-at-oru/spiritual-life/prayer-tower/index.php
richardroberts.org/our-history

A Geodesic Dome with Gilded History
travelok.com/listings/view.profile/id.14567
oklahoman.com/story/news/2021/04/10/renovation-plans-for-oklahoma-city-gold-dome-include-patios-stages/7138643002
okhistory.org/shpo/docs/POKJul2002.pdf
vegaarchitecture.com/work-2/blog-post-title-one-cbkle-t758p-dcl86-9wdle
oklahoman.com/story/news/2002/07/06/history-channel-looks-at-gold-dome/62088570007
nps.gov/places/milk-bottle-grocery.htm

Oklahoma's Nordic Stonehenge
heavenerrunestonepark.com/
travelok.com/listings/view.profile/id.3398
okhistory.org/publications/enc/entry?entry=HE007

A Taste of Pioneer Past
travelok.com/listings/view.profile/id.3342
har-bervillage.com
grandlakeliving.com/attractions-museums/har-ber-village
oklahoman.com/story/news/1983/09/25/har-ber-village-a-trip/62830351007

The Land-Locked Lighthouse
oklahoman.com/story/news/2022/10/02/lake-hefner-lighthouse-oklahoma-city-history/69494982007
oklahomawonders.com/lake-hefner-lighthouse-oklahoma-city-ok
visitokc.com/things-to-do/outdoor-recreation/lake-hefner
blogoklahoma.us/place/575/beckham/centennial-lighthouse

Desert Dunes in the Plains
travelok.com/state-parks/little-sahara-state-park
okhistory.org/publications/enc/entry?entry=LI017
wanderwisdom.com/travel-destinations/Little-Sahara-State-Park-Oklahoma
405magazine.com/a-big-idea-little-sahara/
travelok.com/articles/oklahomasdiverseecoregions
travelok.com/listings/view.profile/id.13372

A Grave Fit for a Horse
travelok.com/listings/view.profile/id.22825
atlasobscura.com/places/mister-eds-grave
kgou.org/oklahoma-news/2019-04-29/how-curious-is-mister-ed-buried-in-oklahoma
greencountryok.com/listing/mister-eds-gravesite/95/#:~:text=His%20resting%20place%20is%20marked,to%20say%20hello%20upon%20arriving.

horseproperties.net/state/oklahoma#:~:text=Oklahoma%20has%20a%20horse%20population,human%2Dto%2Dhorse%20ratio.

No Man's Land
nmlhs.org
travelok.com/listings/view.profile/id.5354
atlasobscura.com/places/no-man-s-land-historical-museum
cntraveler.com/stories/2015-08-04/the-secret-history-of-the-oklahoma-panhandle
okhistory.org/publications/enc/entry?entry=NO001#:~:text=It%20was%20identified%20on%20most,by%20Comanche%20bands%20and%20allied
hmdb.org/m.asp?m=131421

A Tall Drink of Soda
pops66.com
adventureroad.com/destinations/pops-66-soda-ranch-arcadia
travelok.com/listings/view.profile/id.6074
metrofamilymagazine.com/5-things-you-never-knew-about-pops
wanderwisdom.com/travel-destinations/Pops-on-Route-66-The-Worlds-Largest-Soda-Bottle
atlasobscura.com/places/pops
quirkytravelguy.com/quirky-attraction-pops-soda-flavors-route-66-oklahoma

Frank Lloyd Wright's Tallest Masterpiece
pricetower.org
franklloydwright.org/site/price-tower/
travelok.com/listings/view.profile/id.2868
visitbartlesville.com/price-tower-frank-lloyd-wright-architect-bartlesville-ok-listing-389
oklahoman.com/story/business/real-estate/2015/06/01/richard-mize-price-tower-un-world-heritage-site/60742881007
oklahoman.com/story/business/real-estate/2014/01/25/the-classen-tower-in-oklahoma-city-celebrates-its-first-decade/60849860007

Olympic Rapids in the Plains
riversportokc.org
travelok.com/listings/view.profile/id.1314
riversportokc.org/training-site
okctalk.com/showthread.php?t=47637
405magazine.com/metro-athletes-train-for-olympic-gold
kunm.org/local-news/2022-11-11/remembering-first-native-american-to-win-an-olympic-gold-medal-jim-thorpe

Oklahoma's Star Astronaut
staffordmuseum.org
nasa.gov/wp-content/uploads/2016/01/stafford_thomas.pdf?emrc=077c78
cityofweatherford.com/stafford-air-space-museum
airandspace.si.edu/stories/editorial/thomas-stafford
britannica.com/story/how-many-people-have-been-to-the-moon
oklahoma.gov/aerospace/outreach-advocacy/newsroom/remembering-lt-general-thomas-p-stafford-a-true-pioneer-in-air-and-space.html

A Cave for Outlaws
travelok.com/state-parks/robbers-cave-state-park
robberscavestatepark.com
travelok.com/articles/your-complete-guide-to-robbers-cave-state-park
okhistory.org/publications/enc/entry?entry=RO002
owlcation.com/humanities/RobbersCave
owlcation.com/humanities/Jesse-James-Outlaw-Treasure-Tales-of-Oklahoma#:~:text=Legends%20say%20that%20after%20many,gold%20scattered%20throughout%20the%20state.
travelok.com/listings/view.profile/id.17837

A Distillery with a Prohibitionist Past
okhistory.org/publications/enc/entry?entry=NA006
britannica.com/place/Guthrie-Oklahoma
405magazine.com/a-sip-of-history-with-guthries-the-wander-inn
wanderfolkspirits.com
blogoklahoma.us/place/631/logan/same-old-moses-saloon#:~:text=During%20the%2017%20Territorial%20years,stand%20at%20218%20West%20Oklahoma.

The Skinniest Stretch of Route 66
theroute-66.com/ribbon-road-us66.html#-google_vignette
visitmiamiok.com/amenities/tours/ribbon-road
oklahomaroute66.com/ribbon
atlasobscura.com/places/route-66-sidewalk-highway
405magazine.com/route-66s-ribbon-road

Jurassic Museum
samnoblemuseum.ou.edu
okhistory.org/publications/enc/entry?entry=SA014

travelok.com/listings/view.profile/id.6590
okhistory.org/publications/enc/entry?entry=NO004
stwnewspress.com/news/oklahoma-was-once-home-to-some-of-the-largest-dinosaurs-on-the-fossil-record/article_1ced4e29-aecf-5734-8cab-38c838f2cf94.html
travelok.com/listings/view.profile/id.2245
ou.edu/fjjma

Land of 10,000 (Manmade) Lakes
405magazine.com/oklahomyths-shoreline-sadness
oklahoman.com/story/news/2007/11/23/100-amazing-facts-about-oklahoma/61669830007/
onlyinyourstate.com/oklahoma/15-incredible-facts-ok
travelok.com/lakes_and_boating
okhistory.org/publications/enc/entry?entry=LA010#:~:text=Tributaries%20to%20the%20Red%20River,them%20are%20among%20the%20twenty
stateimpact.npr.org/oklahoma/2012/09/27/why-oklahoma-built-more-lakes-than-any-other-state
onlyinyourstate.com/oklahoma/youd-never-guess-ok
okhistory.org/publications/enc/entry?entry=LA010
travelok.com/articles/oklahomas-big-three#:~:text=Eufaula%2C%20Grand%20and%20Tenkiller%20are,the%20waves%20of%20Lake%20Eufaula.
travelok.com/state-parks/lake-thunderbird-state-park
http://oklake.org/about.html
okhistory.org/publications/enc/entry?entry=LA007

Tracing the Ozark Trail
travelok.com/articles/tour-the-ozark-trail-in-oklahoma
okhistory.org/publications/enc/entry?entry=OZ005
oklahomaroute66.com/ozark-trails-obelisk
rd.com/list/state-foods
statesymbolsusa.org/symbol-official-item/oklahoma/state-food-agriculture-symbol/milk
islaskitchenok.com

Oklahoma's Most Haunted Hotel
skirvinhilton.com/history
historichotels.org/us/hotels-resorts/the-skirvin-hilton-oklahoma-city/history.php
bbc.com/travel/article/20211028-the-skirvin-the-us-most-haunted-hotel
oklahoman.com/story/business/columns/steve-lackmeyer/2019/01/29/skirvin-ghost-tales-may-get-a-hollywood-treatment/60475775007
legendsofamerica.com/ok-skirvinhotel/

Solitary Sod House
okhistory.org/sites/sodhouse
travelok.com/listings/view.profile/id.6960
okhistory.org/publications/enc/entry?entry=SO002
atlasobscura.com/places/sod-house-museum
oklahoman.com/story/news/1987/05/24/sod-house-built-to-last-restored-soddie-on-display/62689012007
okmag.com/blog/the-power-of-sod/
okhistory.org/calendar/event/sod-house-museum-50th-anniversary-sod-house-museum/

Roots Run Deep at This Tall Prairie
nature.org/en-us/get-involved/how-to-help/places-we-protect/tallgrass-prairie-preserve
travelok.com/listings/view.profile/id.7647
visittheusa.com/experience/visiting-oklahomas-tallgrass-prairie-preserve

A Barn Built for Dancing
travelok.com/listings/view.profile/id.6497
arcadiaroundbarn.com
nps.gov/places/arcadia-round-barn.htm

Custer's Second-to-Last Stand
nps.gov/waba/index.htm
travelok.com/listings/view.profile/id.8400
wnpa.org/discover_parks/washita-battlefield
okhistory.org/publications/enc/entry?entry=WA037
nps.gov/waba/learn/historyculture/lt-col-george-a-custer.htm
blogoklahoma.us/place.aspx?id=384
nps.gov/trte/planyourvisit/oklahoma.htm

The King Tut of Oklahoma
okhistory.org/sites/spiromounds
okhistory.org/publications/enc/entry?entry=SP012
travelok.com/listings/view.profile/id.7170
bbc.com/travel/article/20210621-spiro-mounds-north-americas-lost-civilisation

The First American Martyr
rothershrine.org
travelok.com/articles/the-blessed-stanley-rother-shrine-what-to-do-see-while-youre-in-oklahoma-city
oklahoman.com/story/news/2023/02/17/blessed-stanley-rother-shrine-dedication-okc-oklahoma-city-friday-feb-17/69859598007

visitokc.com/blog/all-posts/post/visit-the-blessed-stanley-rother-shrine-and-museum
stanleyrotherproject.org/more-about-fr-stanley

Inside Scoop on *The Outsiders* House
theoutsidershouse.com
travelok.com/listings/view.profile/id.28458
visittulsa.com/listing/the-outsiders-house-museum/1963
oklahoman.com/story/entertainment/2023/03/24/the-outsiders-house-museum-filming-locations-important-places-oklahoma-tulsa-windrixville/70042681007
newterritorymag.com/literary-landscapes/s-e-hinton-tulsa-oklahoma

A Museum Fit for Tornado Alley
ou.edu/nwc/partners
ou.edu/nwc
ou.edu/nwc/nwf#:~:text=The%20NWF%20is%20a%20fun,Park%20from%204pm%20to%208pm.
travelok.com/listings/view.profile/id.19225
weather.com/storms/tornado/news/2024-05-02-oklahoma-city-1999-tornado-outbreak
travelok.com/listings/view.profile/id.8260

Oklahoma's Camelot
travelok.com/listings/view.profile/id.23268
atlasobscura.com/places/collings-castle
abandonedok.com/collings-castle
turnerfallspark.com
oklahoman.com/story/news/nation-world/2011/06/12/a-castle-beyond-its-time/61157051007

A Mansion Older Than Statehood
overholsermansion.org
okhistory.org/sites/overholsermansion
oklahoman.com/story/lifestyle/2019/10/21/overholser-mansion-in-okc-still-has-scary-tales/60426913007
okhistory.org/publications/enc/entry?entry=OV003
metrolibrary.org/archives/essay/2019/07/overholser-mansion-jewel-prairie#:~:text=The%20twenty%20rooms%20are%20fitted,National%20Register%20of%20Historic%20Places.

A Road Trip for a Ferris Wheel
wheelerdistrict.com/history-of-the-wheeler-district-ferris-wheel
atlasobscura.com/places/wheeler-ferris-wheel#:~:text=For%20years%20this%20classic%20Ferris,south%20of%20the%20Oklahoma%20River.
pacpark.com/ferris-wheel-125th-anniversary
pacpark.com/films-and-tv-shows-filmed-at-the-santa-monica-pier-in-california
oklahoman.com/story/business/columns/steve-lackmeyer/2019/05/17/in-okc-wheeler-neighborhood-takes-flight/60455401007

The "Bandit Queen's" Demise
atlasobscura.com/places/youngers-bend
blogoklahoma.us/place/898/muskogee/youngers-bend
titchenal.com/Cherokee/chapter3/page09.html
encyclopediaofarkansas.net/entries/belle-starr-2406/#:~:text=Starr's%20life%20of%20crime%20ended,Belle%20Starr%20was%20never%20identified.
okhistory.org/publications/enc/entry?entry=ST018#:~:text=During%20the%20early%201880s%20their,of%20a%20horse%20in%201882.
nps.gov/fosm/learn/historyculture/belle-starr-a-black-widow.htm

Old Jerusalem, Old Mountains
travelok.com/listings/view.profile/id.3595
theholycityofthewichitas.org
okhistory.org/publications/enc/entry?entry=HO018
atlasobscura.com/places/holy-city-of-the-wichitas

Wonders of the Bovine World
okhistory.org/publications/enc/entry?entry=CH045
travelok.com/articles/road-trip-the-chisholm-trail
onthechisholmtrail.com
okhistory.org/publications/enc/entry?entry=CH067
blogoklahoma.us/place/473/blaine/jesse-chisholm
travelok.com/listings/view.profile/id.3935
travelok.com/listings/view.profile/id.22474

A Do-Over for the "World's Greatest Athlete"
atlasobscura.com/places/jim-thorpe-museum-oklahoma
yaleok.org/history-of-yale/jim-thorpe-house/
oklahomasportshalloffame.org/jim-thorpe-museum

Oklahoma's Loch Ness Monster
cryptidz.fandom.com/wiki/Oklahoma_Octopus
cryptozoologycryptids.fandom.com/wiki/Oklahoma_Octopus
onlyinyourstate.com/nature/oklahoma/leg-

end-of-octopus-ok
incertaesedisblog.wordpress.com/2024/05/18/solving-the-case-of-the-oklahoma-octopus
imdb.com/title/tt32369809
travelok.com/state-parks/lake-thunderbird-state-park

The "Indian Capital of the Nation"
travelok.com/articles/a-day-in-anadarko-experience-native-american-history-culture
okmag.com/blog/alluring-anadarko
travelok.com/anadarko
okhistory.org/publications/enc/entry?entry=AN001
cityofanadarko.org
americanindianhof.com
redearth.org/pages/red-earth-festival?srsltid=AfmBOop7aHwyZi583253PiyiTpj4kN_s6oagBeyq761idqhrrfEHrVil
travelok.com/listings/view.profile/id.19072

The Very First Girl Scout Cookie
gswestok.org/en/Programs/cookies/Cookie-History.html#:~:text=It%20all%20started%20in%201917,home%20in%20their%20own%20kitchens.
roadsideamerica.com/story/18578
439529332965434473.weebly.com
vox.com/the-goods/2019/1/24/18195824/girl-scout-cookies-explained-thin-mints-buy

Main Street Oil Well, USA
atlasobscura.com/places/worlds-only-main-street-oil-well
roadsideamerica.com/tip/8695
travelok.com/listings/view.profile/id.4758
onlyinyourstate.com/experiences/oklahoma/small-town-claim-to-fame-ok
npgallery.nps.gov/NRHP/GetAsset/23a130c0-7cb6-441d-a871-219623f30905/?branding=NRHP
travelok.com/listings/view.profile/id.565

Alleyway Art Gallery
plazawalls.org
visitokc.com/listing/plaza-walls/5202/
travelok.com/listings/view.profile/id.23517
artsandculture.google.com/story/plaza-walls-the-beginning-oklahoma-mural-syndicate/7QUBhnhDGwKPLg?hl=en
koco.com/article/oklahoma-city-best-street-art/40664142

Oklahoma's Nuttiest Food Festival
okmulgeechamber.org/pecan-festival
travelok.com/listings/view.profile/id.10449
oklahoman.com/story/news/1989/06/08/okmulgee-plans-on-slice-of-world-pecan-pie-record/62611336007
yourokmulgee.com/2024/09/13/pecan-fest-tradition-continues
swoknews.com/styles/garden/growing-pecans-in-oklahoma/article_713d1ecd-da52-5beb-bc74-9ba9ade86439.html
extension.okstate.edu/articles/2024/oklahoma-pecans.html
edibleoklahomacity.ediblecommunities.com/food-thought/true-natives
extension.okstate.edu/fact-sheets/pecan-varieties-for-oklahoma.html
okhistory.org/publications/enc/entry?entry=PE025
piejunkie.com/our-pies

Oklahoma's Oldest Town Is Electrifying
tulsahistory.org/exhibit/history-is-electric-pso-celebrates-100-years/#:~:text=In%201889%2C%2018%20years%20before,Coalgate%2C%20Lehigh%2C%20and%20 Guthrie.
cherokeephoenix.org/news/vinita-approaches-145-years-of-township/article_fd5e505a-7fac-5d0f-a2b6-8419ce7451e2.html
okhistory.org/publications/enc/entry?entry=VI009
legendsofamerica.com/ok-vinita
easterntrailsmuseum.org
aoc.gov/explore-capitol-campus/art/vinnie-ream

The Cow-Chip-Throwing Capital
espn.com/espn/page2/story?page=rovell/050422&num=0#:~:text=Beaver%20is%20now%20the%20%22Cow,local%20paper%2C%20the%20Beaver%20Democrat.
roadsideamerica.com/story/2188
whisw.blogspot.com/2016/12/beaver-oklahoma-cow-chip-capital-of.html
bon-voyage.co.uk/activities/cow_chip_throwing_capital_of_the_world_beaver_oklahoma#:~:text=Only%20in%20America%20%2D%20Cow%20Chip,%E2%80%9CFrisbee%20of%20the%20Prairie%E2%80%9D.
beaverokchamber.com
rove.me/to/oklahoma/world-cow-chip-throwing-contest
oklahoman.com/story/news/1998/04/05/oklahoma-full-of-cow-chips-cookies-that-is/62286153007
oklahoman.com/story/business/2015/05/12/edmond-man-breaks-cow-chip-throwing-record-in-beaver/60747383007/#:~:text=EDMOND%20%E2%80%94%20Drew%20Russell%20is%20the,Beaver%20County%20Chamber%20of%20Commerce.

A Hippopotamus for Christmas
visitokc.com/articles/post/sing-along-with-oklahoma-city-native-gayla-peevey-for-70th-anniversary-of-hit-song
kjrh.com/news/local-news/from-okc-to-holiday-classic-the-history-behind-i-want-a-hippopotamus-for-christmas-#google_vignette
oklahoman.com/story/entertainment/2024/12/22/okc-zoo-planning-statue-of-i-want-a-hippopotamus-for-christmas-singer/76905195007/#:~:text=Capitalizing%20on%20the%20popularity%20of,the%20wild%20story%20behind%20it.%E2%80%9D
okhistory.org/publications/enc/entry?entry=PE026
news9.com/story/672bb6ee3785e885626caa6a/queen-of-christmas-gayla-peevey-to-return-to-okc-zoo-for-sing-along-event
kgou.org/show/how-curious/2023-11-07/which-oklahoman-got-a-hippopotamus-for-christmas

Calf Fry Country
calffry.com/calffry
cskmedia2015.wordpress.com/2013/05/03/cattlemens-lamb-fries-history-and-how-they-are-made
travelok.com/listings/view.profile/id.19900
tastingtable.com/1737331/what-are-oklahoma-lamb-fries
atlasobscura.com/foods/lamb-fries-testicles-west
okgazette.com/food-drink/balls-out-2964261
cityofvinita.com/events/events/3521
greencountryok.com/event/worlds-largest-calf-fry-festival-%26-cook-off-2024/723/#:~:text=Price:%20Admission:%20$18%20Time:%2011:00%20AM
waggonercowboys.com/original_sack_lunch/#:~:text=Calf%20Fries%20on%20the%20Waggoner,This%20will%20be%20supper.

A statue of Mary overlooks the Blessed Stanley Rother Shrine in Oklahoma City. Courtesy of Visit OKC

INDEX